Dale's Journey

Receiving Inspiration From Our Own Mortality

Dale Pierce and Angie Pierce

Dale's Journey

Cover photo by Brock Kryton Photography

tellwell

Tellwell Talent
www.tellwell.ca

ISBN
978-1-77302-325-0 (Hardcover)
978-1-77302-324-3 (Paperback)
978-1-77302-326-7 (eBook)

Introduction

You are about to accompany us on Dale's Journey, a road that I traveled with my beloved husband. It is a long and winding road with ups and downs, twists and turns, laughter and tears. If yours is a similar path, my heart goes out to you, and I can only hope that by sharing our journey we can make your burden a bit lighter.

Shortly after being diagnosed with terminal pancreatic cancer Dale made the decision to share his journey on Facebook. An unusual choice perhaps, but he never once regretted it. For the most part he posted daily, sometimes he just gave the facts around the day's happenings, his protocols and medical information. If that's all there was to this story I can assure you it would not have gone to print. Dale had an extraordinary amount of wisdom to share and so many of his writings were extremely thought provoking, and based on the response from his "followers" it was very well received. I promised that I would make this book a reality and add my experiences to it. I periodically posted things about our situation on Facebook however I was far too busy to do so on a regular basis. And, I felt the need to keep some of my feelings to myself, at least for the time being.

Dale was a very active and healthy person prior to the symptoms that led to the diagnosis. He was six feet tall and weighed 180 lbs. As his condition deteriorated he found himself unable to do very much, so reflecting on his life, and spending time on the laptop writing was tremendously cathartic. As I've gone through the process of reviewing his posts, and adding my thoughts to it, I have found it to be both excruciating as well as cathartic. One of the things we learned together was that facing the difficult emotions, and working through them is worth the pain. Leaving them just under the surface allows them to fester, and to pop up unannounced, at a later time.

Dale's posts appear here exactly as they did on Facebook. There are some things included that he did not post and there are many responses included. His posts are preceded by his name and the date, and my thoughts are preceded by my name, Angie. Unless specified, my thoughts were not posted on Facebook.

Happy Trails,
Angie

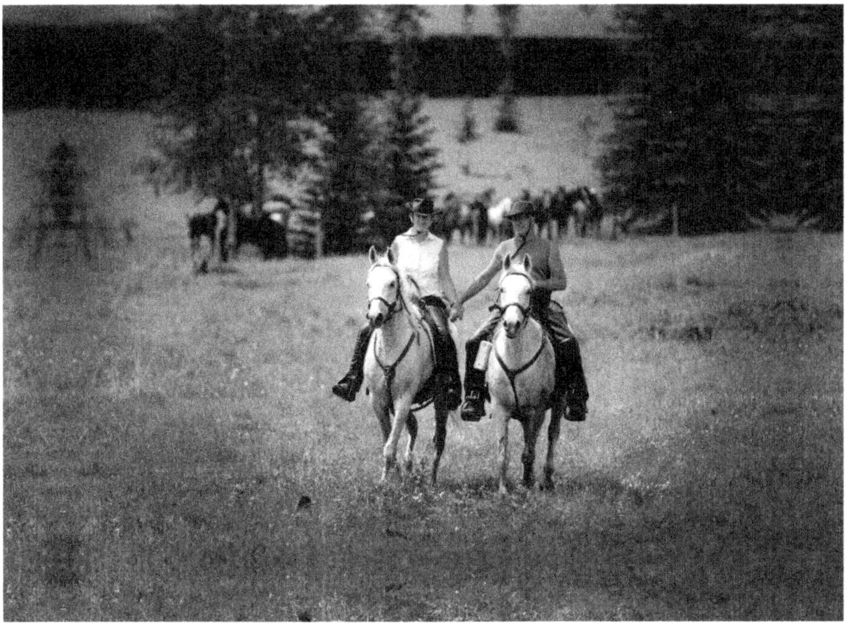

You can connect from all kinds of places- energetic harmony, sexual alchemy, intellectual alignment- but they won't sustain love over a lifetime. You need a thread that goes deeper, that moves below and beyond the shifting sands of compatibility. That thread is fascination- a genuine fascination with someone's inner world, the way they organize reality, the way they hearticulate their feelings, the unfathomable and bottomless depths of their being. To hear their soul cry out to you again and again, and to never lose interest in what it is trying to convey. If there is that, then there will still be love when the body sickens, when the sexuality fades, when the perfection projection is long shattered. If there is that, you will swim in love's waters until the very last breath.

—an excerpt from 'An Uncommon Bond' by Jeff Brown

Epigraph–

"Love allows understanding to dawn, and understanding is precious. Where you are understood, you are at home. Understanding nourishes belonging. When you really feel understood, you feel free to release yourself into the trust and shelter of the other person's soul."

—*John O'Donohue, Anam Cara: A Book of Celtic Wisdom*

Healing is a matter of
TIME,
but it is sometimes
also a matter of
OPPORTUNITY.
~ Hippocrates
www.TheTruthAboutCancer.com

Angie - December 27, 2015

My only child Cody passed away suddenly just over three weeks ago, we are both still reeling from the shock of this tragedy. Cody was like a son to Dale, he didn't have any children of his own. And Cody thought of Dale as a big brother, someone he could rough house with, share a good laugh with and count on when he needed something. Perhaps because we were grieving we ignored Dale's symptoms, chalking them up to stress. In the end I don't believe it would have made any difference if we had addressed the situation sooner. The symptoms resembled "stomach trouble" or acid reflux, but nothing that we tried offered much in the way of relief. Finally on December 27, when Dale turned a bright neon yellow, we decided to head to the U of A hospital. The emergency department was as busy as a beehive and we spent several hours waiting there. Somewhere between time spent reading, watching the goings on, and contemplation I suddenly had a horrible feeling in my gut that this was much more serious than we had suspected, call it woman's intuition or whatever you like but I knew then, that this would not end well. I teared up at the thought but quickly put it aside choosing to remain positive until further notice.

After x-rays and scans they still wanted to do further testing so at 10:00 PM they admitted Dale, and so, with a heavy heart, I went home to take care of our animals.

When I spoke with Dale on the phone early the next morning he didn't say anything about what they'd found, he was saving that bit of info for an in person discussion.

Angie - December 28, 2015

When I got to Dale's room they had him stuffed between the two beds meant for the room. The hospital was so overcrowded that they had to improvise to make space. He took my hand, and gently told me that they had found a tumour in the pancreas and that it seemed to have spread to the lungs as well. Overcome with shock and sadness we shared a flood of tears. I felt that the tears he cried were for me, and not for his own predicament. Once the initial shock was past, Dale seemed to be resigned to his fate, they really hadn't given him any hope for survival. My reaction to his acceptance was that this was our opportunity to walk our talk and approach this situation in the same way that Dale would recommend to his clients. He would suggest, only if they were open to suggestion of course, that they examine the emotional aspects of the disease and apply protocols that support the body. It was at this time that we began our journey through the nightmare of cancer. We would walk this journey together every step of the way.

Dale - December 31, 2015

I guess it's time to announce that I have been presented with the ultimate opportunity to walk the walk I've been talking for the last few years. This hospital visit started with what looked like gall bladder issues, but there is no longer any doubt that the real cause is tumours. How extensive we're not sure yet, but it's pretty clear this is serious stuff. I have decided to make this journey public. The only thing I'm asking my friends (and anyone else who wants) to do is to use whatever form of energetic connection they have to support our journey. I intend to update this on a daily basis.

Dale - January 1, 2016

Today's good news - they sent me home. Yesterday they did an endoscopy to view the bile duct and try to insert a stent. No luck there - the tumour's too big but they were able to insert a stent in the duodenum so at least my stomach can drain into the small intestine. I'm home now until I get a call Monday from the GI guy about further blood work and an attempt to do a bile duct stent from the outside, and another call from the Cross Cancer Institute for an oncology consult. Apparently surgery is not an option now, so we'll see. As many of you already know, I am totally against chemo. Today I received a much appreciated and intense Reiki treatment from two very dear people. I'm still processing that. I just finished Dr. Joe Dispenza's book "You Are the Placebo" and started the meditations today, it just makes so much sense. This seems like the beginning of my real life.

Angie

While I was waiting for Dale to be finished with the procedure I spent some time on Facebook, I felt as though I'd been punched in the stomach when I read the shocking and incredibly sad news that Fraser Holmes had passed away after a brief recurrence with leukemia. He played at our wedding celebration with Amanda Rheaume and was only in his 20s.

Dale - January 2, 2016

Researching alternative cures today, and continuing to feel better each hour on my diet of Frankincense oil orally every two hours, fresh organic fruit and vegetables juiced every couple of hours (still small stomach capacity), daily dry sauna for detox, and very soon a lovely bowl of rice congee. Research continues, and a few things are on their way to us. I also looked briefly at the Hoffman Institute in Calgary, but they may be too slow moving for me (I'm not sure I can wait three months for treatment to start).

Dale - January 3, 2016

Latest research on pancreatic cancer says that with chemo, survival rate is 7–8% (1 out of 14), while with Gerson Therapy (which is part of what I'm doing) survival rate is 50%. Add to that quality of life (which, in my book, is more crucial than quantity) and there is no question about which route I'm going. Which way would you choose to go? I also have the prayers and energy support of some of the most wonderful people in the world, plus three other aces up my sleeve. I feel like whichever way this goes, I'm doing the right thing and I'm totally prepared to accept the consequences of my choices. Today I felt strong enough to complete the whole Pal Dan Gum routine. I felt a little tired afterwards, but better than yesterday mentally and physically. I also tried a little gravity inversion to see if I could relieve the pressure on the bile duct. I'm looking forward to seeing a few clients tomorrow, spaced a little more widely than usual.

Angie

I am now somewhat dubious of the 50% success rate that the Gerson Therapy offered, based on what we inevitably learned about pancreatic cancer. I am not sure where Dale got those stats.

Dale taught classes in Pal Dan Gum which is similar to Tai Chi but involves only the Eight Silken Movements.

Dale - January 4, 2016

I have been so blessed by all the messages of support and love that I have received since I went public with this, but I have also been slightly disturbed by the number of people who know me and think I need sympathy. Sympathy is for victims and I AM NOT A VICTIM! This is an event in my journey. It may be a challenge, and it most assuredly is an opportunity. Nobody did this to me. I do not hate God, or the Universal Force, or Big Pharma, or Monsanto, or the commercial food industry for messing me up. Live or die, I am victorious, because I have not lost myself in this event. Send love, send support, send energy in all of its forms, but please (and I don't mean to be rude here) save your sympathy for someone who needs it.

Dale - January 5, 2016

Feeling good again today. Started with a 50 minute meditation in a 53 degree Celsius infrared sauna, juicing, oatmeal, frankincense, and then off to the city for my 9:00 AM appointment for 45,000 mg of vitamin C intravenous at Dr. Steinke's (Naturopath) office. Did a little more research today and saw a couple of clients, juice and soup, felt pretty beat so called it a day (except went shopping with Angie on the way home). More juice and then hallelujah – a two-egg omelet (no spices☹). I feel like my days are so full, never a time when I'm not doing something out of my protocols, but I feel healthier every day. The ER doctor called me at home today to see how I was doing, he's an amazing guy who impressed me hugely on Sunday. Well, off to my castor oil heat pack, another juice, a little gravity inversion, essiac tea and a little meditation before bed.

Dale - January 6, 2016

I had a poor night last night, maybe almost that "dark night of the soul" that I've read about, but we got through it. Might have been something I ate or didn't eat yesterday, so I'll add some things and drop some others and see where we go. OMG! I had coffee this morning. The aroma of it being brewed was like visiting heaven – lovely organic full flavored roast. Flavor-wise, eh. Never got to taste it. BUT when the caffeine hit my bloodstream, wow! I believe that the whole experience rejuvenated my liver just a little, and I really felt and looked (according to Angie) better almost immediately. Now that we have the logistics of coffee enemas figured out, it should go even smoother tomorrow. I then went on to have a pretty good day. A couple of clients that brightened my horizon and left me feeling stronger after their treatments than I felt before. Added digestive enzymes today, and continue to move forward on a few other avenues, I just keep feeling more positive every day.

Angie

Making coffee enemas takes some skill! Getting the temperature perfect is a challenge, and making sure there are no grounds is also important.

We also eventually learned that carbohydrates feed cancer, so the oatmeal and rice congee were not the best choices. There is an incredible amount of information available however it takes real detective skills to sift through it and find the best solutions.

Dale - January 7, 2016

Better night last night – trying to stuff enough calories into my shrunken stomach to maintain 155 lbs. is a fine balancing act, but we seem to be making progress. Morning coffee (nudge, nudge, wink, wink) followed by a trip into the city for my 45,000 mg vitamin C IV. Juicing, smoothie with enzymes, essiac tea, keeping track and keeping on schedule are the hardest parts. Two clients today – just so I don't get too rusty, and then some writing to help me put things into perspective. Feeling pretty good this evening. Probably watch a bit of Idol and hit the sack before 10:00.

Dale - January 8, 2016

The Enerchi Massage newsletter went out yesterday, and today I received a number of messages and cards from clients and friends that literally opened my heart. Thank you to everyone who took the time to write, and also to those who took the time to send healing or love. I'm having an even better day today, and have eaten more without pain than since Dec. 23. I am blessed. Yesterday I added Turmeric Oil, wheatgrass and a 17 mushroom blend.

Angie

The 17 mushroom blend was to support Dale's immune system. It's interesting to note that even though he was in and out of hospitals for six months, he never developed so much as a sniffle.

Dale - January 9, 2016

Since radiation and chemotherapy are the only two approved treatments for cancer, it's important to let people know that other options do exist. If you want to be healthy, you must explore your options and find out more information about them so YOU can make the best possible choice for yourself. It's always important to do your own research. And just so I'm clear, this is only one of many possible solutions that have demonstrated good results. It is also very important to understand that no cancer gets permanently cured without dealing with the spiritual and emotional causes of disease in the body.

Today was a day for some new things, especially because I could spend the whole day on me. I'm carrying on with all of the protocols we've talked about so far, but started the day with a lemon cleanse to set me up for the daily coffee. That was valuable. Also today, I received a lovely hot stone massage from my own personal angel, and that left me feeling pretty good. Shortly I will have my third meal of the day, for the second day in a row, as well as the juicing, and I am feeling stronger every day. Still writing and meditating, working through some old stuff, and finally revisiting Signature Cell Healing for its potential.

Angie

We found that sometimes the coffee enema was hard for Dale to retain because it served as a cleanser. That's why we resorted to using the lemon first so that he'd be able to retain the coffee for 15 minutes. This process of meeting Dale's needs involved a whole lot of trial and error.

I must say that I always felt appreciated. Dale made a point of letting me know how much he loved me and that he was grateful for my efforts in caring for him.

Regarding the protocols we used to support Dale's body, certain things were extremely costly. The GcMAF for instance would not have been a possibility if we hadn't been able to borrow a very large sum of money from some wonderful friends. I believe that in certain cases it has been successful in stopping the growth of tumours but pancreatic cancer is a tough one. Vitamin C IVs are fairly costly but they certainly help with the general sense of well-being, they are quite often combined with chemo to offset the side effects.

It is my belief that organic produce is the only way to go, especially for juicing. Root vegetables take on the most chemicals and carrots and beets are the staples of juicing. The cost of organic produce is higher but the nutritional quality and the taste are better. The stats on cancer are now one in two people, there's got to be some problems with what we are consuming, and if you look at the chemicals used in farming these days there must be a correlation. I feel that with every dollar I spend I make the conscious choice to become a part of the solution rather than a part of the problem.

The juicer itself is also worth investing in. We had a $100 model but with Dale's diagnosis we invested in a $380 model. The difference was huge! Dale said with the cheaper one the juice was like Kool-Aid compared to the flavorful version the expensive model produced. The waste was substantially less with the better juicer as well, which helps offset the cost.

The countless supplements that are available can add up at the cash register. I'd suggest doing your research, thoroughly. There are many things that claim to make a difference, but not so many that back it up with evidence. We often relied on muscle testing (Applied Kinesiology) to help us decide whether or not to try something when we weren't certain. Whether or not it's accurate, we have relied on muscle testing for many years.

If you're looking after yourself, or someone else at home, cut out the processed foods. You will stop exposing yourself to GMOs and countless chemicals, and you will save money, even if you buy exclusively organic.

And finally, nothing replaces food prepared with love.

Dale - January 10, 2016

What a wonderful quote from Rumi c/o Tina Livingston

This being human is a guest house. Every morning is a new arrival. A joy, a depression, a sadness, a meanness, some momentary awareness comes as an unexpected visitor. Welcome and entertain them all! Even if they're a crowd of sorrows, who violently sweep into your house empty of its furniture, still, treat each guest honorably. He may be clearing you out for some new delight. The dark thought, the shame, the sorrow, the malice, meet them at the door laughing and invite them in. Be grateful for whoever comes, because each has been sent as a guide from beyond. ~ Rumi

Today's new thing was to replace the morning coffee with wheatgrass and liquid kelp, for its nutritional value as well as its anti-cancer properties. The new plan is to alternate days – wheatgrass with kelp one day and coffee with kelp the next. Also, more time today for contemplation, including watching one of Dr. Joe Dispenza's talks from YouTube. Wisdom and personal experience coming together to inspire me in ways I had not thought of. Food wise, I'm eating more each day with less trouble. Still not draining the liver completely, but making progress.

Dale - January 11, 2016

A friend asked me this in a PM, because she didn't want to ask it in public, but I think it is a very good question and so I'm going to answer it here. "Looking back, how long do you think you were symptomatic before you sought out a diagnosis?" The sad thing about pancreatic cancer is that it is probably the least symptomatic cancer to have. That being said, I had some clues in late November, things such as acid reflux (which I've had before) and mild epi-gastric pain, which we were treating. I've also been tired for a few months, which we chalked up to low adrenals, which we were treating.

December 2, Angie's son Cody (whom I grew to love in the last ten years as if he were my own) died suddenly and that put our world off-kilter. As Solstice approached, I was having more and more trouble eating, and from about Dec 20 I could only sleep sitting up. I tried meds and treatment for probable causes based on my past experience, but nothing helped for more than a short while. On Dec. 25 I started to turn slightly yellow, which was the sign that something serious was wrong – I thought gallstones at that point. On the 27th, it was bad enough that I decided (with some encouragement from people who care) to go to U of A emergency. By 3:00 on the 28th, I had a "most responsible diagnosis" of pancreatic cancer, with a tumour large enough to block the bile duct (hence the jaundice) and the duodenum (hence the reflux). They also picked up "suspicious nodes" in the lungs. As we sit and try to figure out why I didn't take more concrete action sooner, the major conclusion I've come to is that I have never believed in my own mortality, and going to the doctor sooner, if they would have even looked past the surface in a guy that was as healthy as me, would have confirmed my mortality. Something to think about.

On another note, today we decided that going to Mexico on the 21st of January just wasn't a good idea, given the state of my health, so we cancelled the trip. The cats and the dog will be quite happy, and I can spend some more time focusing on healing.

Angie

Later on we found out that pancreatic cancer can be present for up to 20 years before presenting any symptoms, even though it appears to come on quickly. I think we would've gone on that holiday if we would have had insurance coverage. It's important to know that when you purchase medical travel insurance for a trip it does not come into effect until the date you leave so any pre-existing conditions can render it null and void.

Dale and Cody in San Francisco in November, 2014.

Dale - January 12, 2016

ON COURAGE

Courage is your willingness to not know.
To speak your truth. To walk your path.
To face ridicule and rejection.
To keep going, despite the voices in your head and the judgements of others.
And there are no guarantees you will make it.

Nobody can walk for you!
You walk in radical aloneness, naked in the face of life, no protection, no crutches, no external authority.
No ideology to save you.
No promises anymore.
Only the beating of the heart, and the air in the lungs, and the
thrill and terror of being utterly free, and no longer numb.

And a knowing from deep within.
And the call of your ancestors.
And the ground holding you.
And the sun nourishing you.

And the fragrance of love everywhere.
And warm tears running down your cheeks.

And this gorgeous vulnerability
which makes you totally unbreakable.

- Jeff Foster

Today I'm doing much better physically and mentally. Yesterday, I had an unexpected experience of the emotion of fear. Having that understanding of my own mortality, finding out my travel insurance would exclude anything possibly related to the cancer as coverable, not being able to eat for the first time since I left the hospital, all left me with a feeling that I truly believed until then that I was immune to, FEAR. So I sat with it for the evening. And I went to bed with it. And I dreamed a little. And I awoke without the fear, and with a sense of the value of allowing my emotions. I feel ready to continue to face this challenge with courage, and with joy, and with a little bit of irreverence.

Dale - January 13, 2016

Feeling even better today, and my appetite is coming back. Still trying to be mindful in my eating, to give my body maximum support. Also, my color is improving, so the liver is draining somewhat (which my G/I guy said should happen), which is a huge relief that I'm not creating more problems while I focus on one or two things. Booked to see a few clients today, and it feels so good to be working, because this work nurtures my soul. The end of the day, 4 clients today in 9 hours is just about the perfect amount of rest time, I feel as good now as I did this morning. Having some thoughts related to the idea of "fighting" cancer, but more about that in the next few days. For now, about to head home and end my day.

Dale - January 14, 2016

Short update on condition: Lost a few more pounds (I even looked under the bed, in case) but feeling good still, food is moving through and that's encouraging. Had a marvelous energy treatment from Chris E. today. If you have an energy imbalance, you really should see her. Going to see Shaman Pete tonight for his talk and group session. Feeling positive.

On another note, I've been struggling with the whole idea of "fighting" cancer. I've always been morally opposed to the concept of doing things "for cancer" (run, walk, ride, etc.) but I find myself thinking deeply on the subject of even being against cancer. After all, what is cancer? In my view, it all boils down to this: Cancer (diagnosed or not) is my body giving me notice that something is not right at some level in me, and I'm not dealing effectively with that thing. We all have cancer cells in our body at any given time, but if conditions become optimal, tumours form. What optimizes conditions? Too many toxins (environmental, food related, alcohol, etc.), and unresolved emotional and spiritual trauma (because that lowers immunity). So, fighting cancer is kind of like shooting the messenger. If I've got stuff to deal with, I'd rather know and have the opportunity to change something. So I'm thanking this tumour for the opportunity to make a change before it's too late. I'm thanking this tumour for the opportunity to see how loved

I am, while I'm still here. I'm thanking this tumour for waking me up. I'm thanking this tumour for the opportunity to do something meaningful, that I believe in. And I'm thanking all of you for your steadfast support and kinder words than I ever expected to hear.

Angie

I was in total agreement with Dale in regards to his perspective on "fighting" cancer as well as his feelings about the "industry". Raising money for so-called research is a joke, Big Pharma gains nothing by finding a cure. Not to mention the billions of dollars they make from selling chemo and the drugs needed to combat the side effects.

Dale - January 15, 2016

Went to a talk and group healing "journey" last night with Shaman Pete Bernard. There must have been about 40 people there, and he talked for about an hour – the whole talk felt like he was giving me a one-on-one session. Followed the talk with the healing journey, and I went deep and far. Thank you shaman Pete and Chris for reminding us. Saw clients today, and the sessions were marvelous. Received a session from Kim McE. in the late afternoon, and now I have lots of food for meditation. Yay. A little behind on the protocols today, I probably over-scheduled myself a bit, but still feeling good about where I am and where I'm going. Good night all, Love, Light and Laughter.

Angie

Shaman Pete spoke of death and dying.

Dale - January 16, 2016

Got a head's up from Samantha on frankincense oil this morning, which I had never questioned this deeply. Research turned up some good information, culminating with this: "So, if you are looking for a natural substance to help prevent or treat cancer, frankincense oil should not be your first choice. Look instead to turmeric/curcumin, to cannabis/cannabinoids, to garlic/garlic oil, and to frankincense extract, which is sold in capsule form. Following that, I would consider essential oils of cinnamon bark, lemongrass, citronella, turmeric, orange, lemon and bergamot. I have not discussed them all here but these have, in my opinion, a better shot than frankincense oil. The only exception seems to be that of skin cancer. After a bit more follow-up and checking of facts, we went on a quest for frankincense extract and were able to track down some 65% boswellic acid extract at Sam's Teas and Spices (online), and have ordered some from there.

On another note, I have something serious to think and meditate about after my session with Kim yesterday. Her session helped me connect a lot of what had seemed like random dots, and explain a lot of things that have gone, and are going, on in my life. I have received so many messages over the past two weeks, and they are all coming together into a common thread, for which I will be ever grateful both to the messengers and the senders. May you all receive the healing you are sending me, multiplied many times over.

Dale - January 17, 2016

Second consecutive day of rest, and I'm feeling good today, in spite of the strong winds I can hear. Angie is really insisting that I take it as easy as possible, and between her looking after all of my needs, and today giving me a hot stone massage, I do not know what I would do without her. Today was a heat day: I had my sauna this morning, I've kept warm all day, and now the hot massage, and then after supper (FISH!) a hot castor oil pack. Going deeper with the non-physical work, and today made some potential progress on the issue raised in my session with Kim yesterday. I am blessed in so many ways, I started a gratitude journal today.

Angie

Dale mentioned that he did not know what he would do without me. He and I had often said in the past that neither of us could imagine life without the other. Sadly, I sometimes did begin to imagine that, but for the most part, my focus was on getting Dale healthy.

Dale and Angie on a competitive trail ride near Brule, Alberta in 2013.

Dale - January 18, 2016

Today was an off day. Pain all day left me feeling a little low, and Angie reminded me that my last bad day was last Monday. I wonder if this is truly the "after-the-weekend" blues? Anyway, some new information on protocols culminated in a decision today to go with the GcMAF hormone treatment instead of the Mexican Laetrile (B17) treatment. Very promising in the literature, and I had a few friends check it out as well, so we are going to try to get some in. No other changes in protocols to report at this time, but am moving forward on the spiritual end steadily, and that is all that I could ask for. Thank you to Cheryl S. for a lovely visit and energy exchange today. Thank you again to all of my friends for sending energy, prayers and wishes.

Dale - January 19, 2016

Better day again, especially after yesterday: that vitamin C recharge with meditation really seems to bring me up each week. Working on the protocols, and trying to make sure not to leave any stone unturned, we continue to research both the things we are doing, and the things we might do. Did a little self-visceral manipulation, to see if I could move the tumour in such a way as to, even momentarily, free up the bile duct and/or the stomach, with some feeling of success. Today I decided not to have the biopsy they want this Friday. The purpose of the biopsy is to determine which type of chemo to use on me. Unfortunately, they are not worried about metastasizing the cancer with this procedure, nor can they give me any assurance that knowing the particular type of cancer this is (one of two varieties) increases my chance of survival with their methods. Add to that eight or nine hours of my time that could be much more productively used. The more I learn, the more I'm sticking to my original position, which is NO TO CHEMO!

Angie

Through our research we discovered that often, cutting into, or taking biopsies speeds the growth of cancer by supplying oxygen to the tumour. When asked what he thought, our naturopath commented "Why poke an angry bear?".

Dale - January 20, 2016

I'm more and more convinced that what I am doing is not a fight. I am in the midst of a discussion between my body, the expression of what I want to do here on earth, and my eternal spirit, which holds the knowledge of what I am here on earth to accomplish. No matter what I do to heal my body, if I don't bring the discussion between my body and spirit to a successful solution, any physical healing can only be temporary, at best. So in all of this, I am doing everything that I can to support my physical body long enough to bring this discussion to a successful conclusion. Then I will have the choice of continuing my mission in this corporeal body or moving on to the next stage in my journey. This understanding simplifies my decision making and continues to provide me with peace and joy even as I experience some things that we generally think of as negative.

Angie

I now believe that bringing this book into existence was part of Dale's mission here. If it helps just a few people, it is worthwhile.

Dale - January 21, 2016

Today I have to relinquish all solid foods until my tumour shrinks enough to allow my stomach to function properly. Angie can now start supplying me with baby-food consistency meals, blenderized especially for me. So if I'm in my second babyhood now, does that mean my second childhood is imminent? Consulted my GP today to get started on the paperwork for a prescription for pain management, so should see something in the next few days. Also today, we decided to go ahead with a hormone being produced in Europe with better result statistics than Laetrile, so jumping through the banking system hoops to get that paid for so they can ship it next week. The hormone is GcMAF (www.gcmaf.se), which is a cancer killer that is found in everybody, but disappears when you get a cancer tumour (or maybe disappears and then you get a tumour?). They think I'll need to be on this for 12 – 18 months, but at a lower dosage once the tumour shrinks, to get complete eradication. I am still grateful to all of my friends sending prayers, good wishes and energy in so many different forms. I have never in my life felt as blessed as I do today.

Dale - January 22, 2016

After my post yesterday I helped Angie wrap and set out three fresh round bales, and I must say I am embarrassed at how weak I am now. Yesterday evening I realized that I was holding a smoldering anger most of the day, and hadn't even noticed it for the most part. I spent some time with a person yesterday who was so stuck in being a victim that every time I steered the conversation away from victim mentality they just went right back to that speech pattern. After an hour of listening to this, I found myself getting angry enough to bluntly ask the other person to quit talking, because I had no energy to listen to what they had to say. I stuffed that anger for the rest of the day until it got brought up again in the evening by something totally unrelated. When I thought about where that came from, I realized that I had a fear of even considering that I was a victim, and a small buried part of me that wanted to call myself a victim. When I sat with that energy for a while, I realized that this thought could pass through my mind without becoming who I am, as long as I'm willing to recognize and then release them. With that, the anger dissipated, and I was able to go to bed and sleep.

Today was a better day emotionally and physically. I spent a bit of time with a client and dear friend this morning, and then my lifelong friend Harry and Lori drove up from Calgary to spend a few hours with us, and it was marvelous. Friendships are so rewarding, every time I spend time with, or communicate with, my friends my vibration raises. I am blessed beyond measure with Angie and the other friends that I have in my life.

Dale - January 23, 2016

Last night was rough again – between the pain and the feeling of distension in my stomach I didn't get to sleep until 2:00 AM, and that was in the lazyboy. The good news is I slept until 10:00 this morning, so I at least got my eight hours. Felt pretty good today, spent an hour riding my horse (first time since November 2), including tacking and untacking all by myself (I'm <u>such</u> a big boy now). Went and saw someone today who basically kicked me in the ass and said "you don't have time to screw around". They are right, I don't have time, and yet I find myself reluctant to focus on my inner work in the same way that I would focus on a client, or on a project on the farm. The ultimate challenge: deal with your fear of success, and do it right now. It's now just past 7:30, and my stomach is giving me trouble again, so I have to assume that I have not yet stopped the growth of the tumour. That tells me that I "don't have time to screw around" and maybe it's time to start taking this cancer thing seriously. We got the GcMAF ordered yesterday, and hope to see it in the coming week. I believe that on the physical level, that will make a big difference, but I **cannot** put off the other work any longer.

Dale - January 24, 2016

Continuing to feel better, and discovered that my body has no capacity whatsoever to digest salmon in particular, and probably all meats. Finally cleared the salmon that I ate Wednesday from my system this morning, and that is not acceptable. Lack of enzymes from the pancreas and a lack of churning action in the stomach has decreed that I shall be Vegan until I get my stomach back at the least. Vegan, and everything pureed. Had a great meditation this morning, and I attribute that to the motivation I received yesterday triggering a shift for me today. I understand some things differently today. Finally, had a lovely visit with my mother, sister and brother-in-law this afternoon and until after 7:00 this evening. I'm not as exhausted after their visit as I expected to be, and that is another good sign. I had intended to answer some personal emails and messages today, but I don't have a lot left so I hope those who are waiting for replies will be patient until tomorrow.

Dale - January 25, 2016

I have discovered that there is something harder to live with than pain, mostly because it's harder to control than pain. I find myself itching from head to toe, 24 hours a day. The worst is when I am just waking up, because my iron self-control has not kicked in yet, and I often wake up to the realization that I have scratched myself to bleeding while I was waking up. I have a very good organic non-chemistry-based cream that stops the itch, and I dare not forget to put it on two or three times daily, and especially just before bed. My body needs nine or ten hours of sleep every night: it is working very hard to heal itself, and so I try to give it every aid that I can to heal. I'm growing to like this body, and would love to have use of it for a while longer. In this vein, I am happy to announce that I feel better today than yesterday.

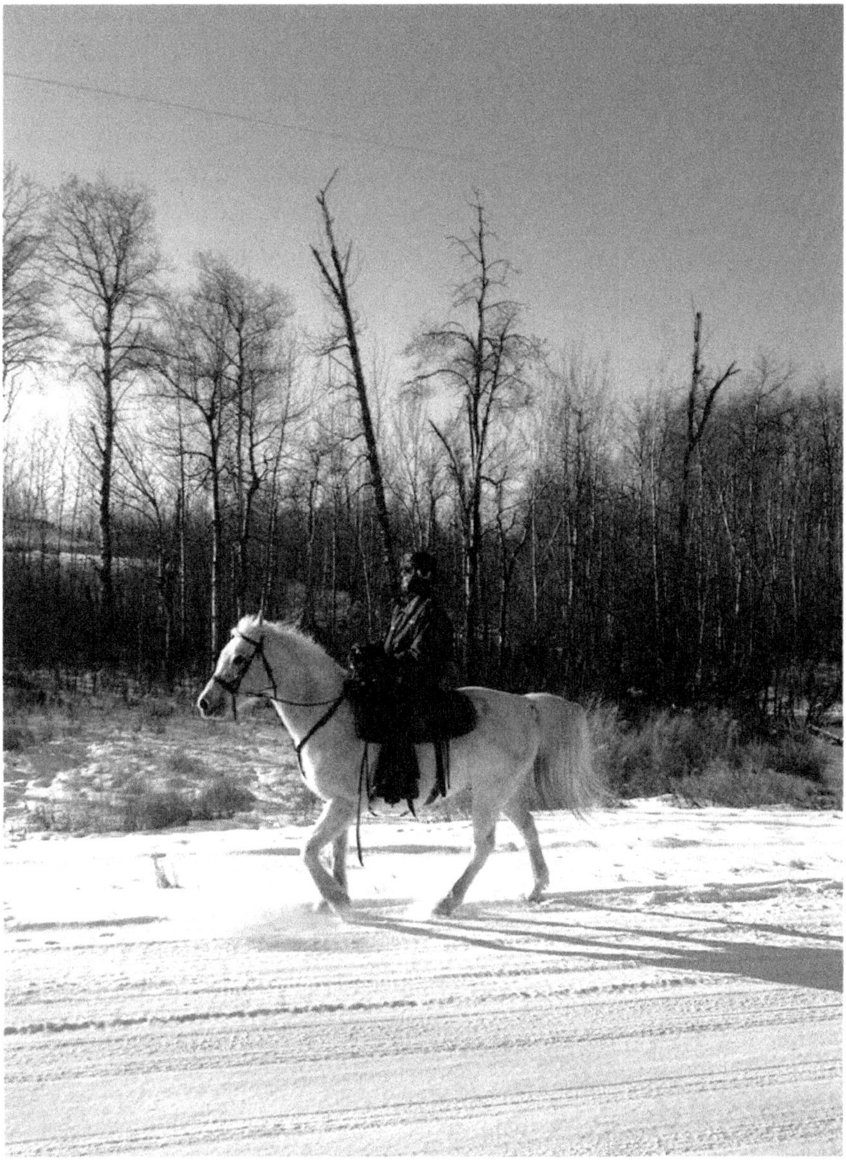

Dale riding Mo on January 23.

On another note, I want to clarify something about my understanding of the medical system. I do not believe that doctors, nurses and other staff are my enemy in this journey. I do believe, however, that Big Pharma is only interested in one thing, and that thing is money. Sadly, most of the information that medical staff receive originates with or is filtered through, Big Pharma. Add in the pressure of "best practice of medicine" interpretations, which seem to threaten doctors with everything from blocked advancement to loss of credentials if they step outside of the "norm", and we end up with a self-perpetuating system that denies the possibility of unusual solutions, especially in the treatment of cancer. My major objection to chemotherapy, which against much of the advice I'm receiving I am refusing, is that it directly supports the paradigm of profit for Big Pharma with little in the way of long term benefits to me. The therapy I'm on has demonstrated results of 75 – 100% cure rates for pancreatic cancer, which is ten times better than the very best numbers for chemo. My solution may well not be for everyone, but there is no doubt in my mind that it is right for me.

Angie

Sadly, I feel that we were misled with the 75 – 100% cure rates for pancreatic cancer promised by one advocate for the GcMAF hormone treatment. When I spoke with a different person there, I was told that they had recently had one success with pancreatic cancer.

Dale - January 26, 2016

We have some amazing friends that have gone above and beyond the call of duty and found ways of making this journey bearable. I won't name all of you, but want to extend special recognition to some of you in no particular order. Dennis and Mary-Lynn D., Shawn St, Josh L., Robin S. (and Mom), Harry and Lori U., Chris E., Dr. Wayne Steinke, Jerry J., Carol L., Daisy S.. People like you make this world a better place to be, and Angie and I thank you from the bottom of our hearts.

Yesterday Angie and I rode our boys again for an hour – that seems like a good distance to go until all four of us are more fit. We both rode in our Tucker saddles for safety's sake, which feel like huge armchairs compared to our endurance saddles, and they are so heavy (relatively) that I think as long as I can get that sucker up onto Mo's back, I deserve to ride. Every ride leaves me feeling more alive.

Dale and Angie at Writing On Stone Provincial Park, competing in the "Rattlesnake Roundup".

This morning I had my appointment at the Cross Cancer Institute, to get some definitive answers about what they can do. As suspected, the purpose of the biopsy which I declined was to determine which type of chemo drug to give me. The news that I didn't expect was that any treatment, including chemo, will be strictly palliative, and the best I can expect with the most aggressive chemo is an extra 5 months, if my liver can be manually drained through a stent between my ribs. The good news is Alberta Health pays for the chemo and the stent. The bad news is I pay for the drugs to counteract the side effects.

That palliative word set me back a bit, as even though I knew my odds within the standard system were not good, I still had the misconception that chemo and surgery after were a possibility with some chance of success. Hearing that I have no choice is a game changer, I can tell you that much, and roundly reaffirms that the choice Angie and I made on January 1 was the right choice. So we will continue to pursue the routes that we have been on and support my body while my soul and spirit get the work they need to bring this all to a successful focus. We are holding out a lot of hope for the new product on its way to us now, and should know within a few weeks if that is working.

Angie

The doctor we saw at the Cross did not look at us like we were nuts when Dale told her that he was not interested in chemo, she simply informed us that it was her role to tell us what they had to offer. To us, it felt like a sales pitch.

All of our research suggests that sugar feeds cancer, interestingly, they offer carts filled with sugar laden snacks at the Cross. And, they suggest that Dale turn to liquid meal replacements like Boost and Ensure to meet his "nutritional requirements". Any of the products like those that I researched are sugar/corn syrup based (about 47%) with added vitamins. A smoothie containing homemade coconut milk, fruit and high quality protein powder can offer the needed calories without refined sugar or corn syrup and no "artificial" ingredients.

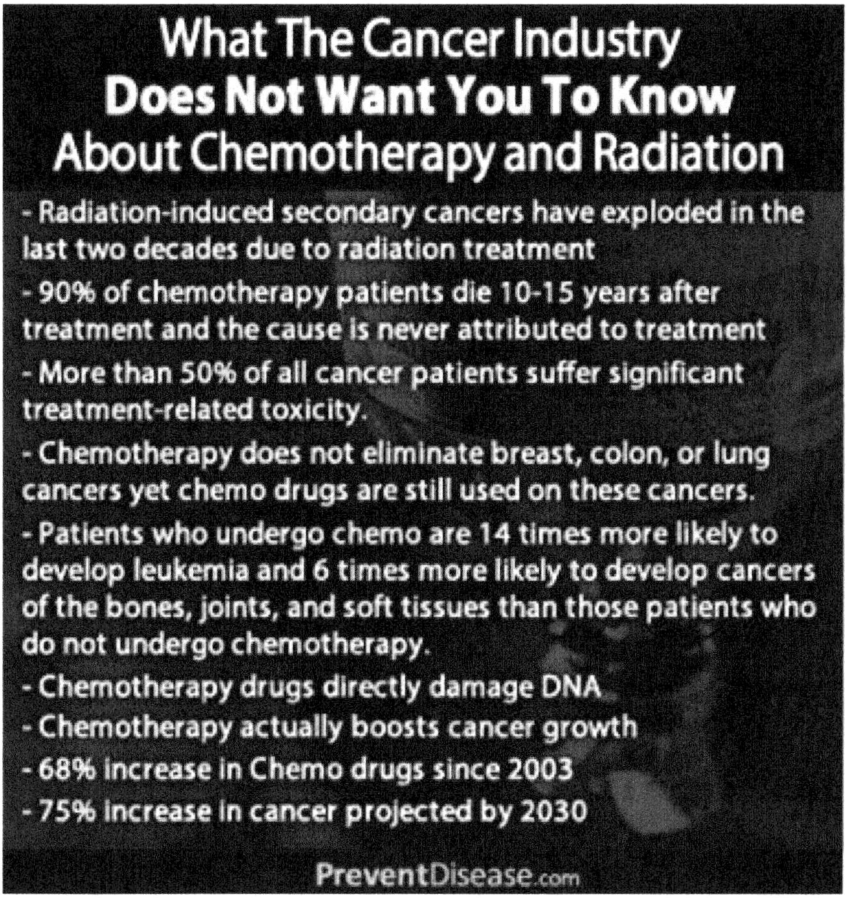
What The Cancer Industry
Does Not Want You To Know
About Chemotherapy and Radiation
- Radiation-induced secondary cancers have exploded in the last two decades due to radiation treatment
- 90% of chemotherapy patients die 10-15 years after treatment and the cause is never attributed to treatment
- More than 50% of all cancer patients suffer significant treatment-related toxicity.
- Chemotherapy does not eliminate breast, colon, or lung cancers yet chemo drugs are still used on these cancers.
- Patients who undergo chemo are 14 times more likely to develop leukemia and 6 times more likely to develop cancers of the bones, joints, and soft tissues than those patients who do not undergo chemotherapy.
- Chemotherapy drugs directly damage DNA
- Chemotherapy actually boosts cancer growth
- 68% increase in Chemo drugs since 2003
- 75% increase in cancer projected by 2030
PreventDisease.com

Dale - January 27, 2016

One of the things that I forgot to mention yesterday was that I am now somewhere between milk and Twinkies... that is to say that I now have an expiry date, which is April 15, 2016, and as macabre as that sounds, having a "best before" date is actually a pretty good motivator. Every day that I am still here past that date is a testament to what we can do if we take responsibility for our health back from "the system". Because of that, we feel that the next month is the critical stage, where we can either turn this around or the damage to my body will be too much to overcome. So that means that I am cutting down even more on clients for the next month at least, asking my city clients to see the other therapists in our clinic whenever they can, and calling or emailing Angie or I directly to get the appointments they need for what only I can deliver, because my online schedule will show not available even though I might be. I don't want any of my clients going wanting while I am rebuilding, but I just cannot physically handle the workload I have carried for the next few months.

Today was another good day on balance. I saw a few clients, and felt pretty good, but I feel like my stomach is resisting the food I want to put into it. It's a fine balancing act to get as many calories as possible while paying attention to not overloading the now much smaller system. Also, I'm starting to have afternoon naps, at all hours of the day. I think that being kept awake by the itching is starting to take its toll, so my body will take every opportunity to make it up. I'm trying a homeopathic itch remedy today, and it is showing some promise, so we'll see. I was given a prescription yesterday for an antihistamine, but when we read up on it, it has the potential side effect of negatively impacting my liver, which is already in enough trouble.

Enerchi Massage and Wellness Centre Newsletter - February edition:

After my visit to the Cross Cancer Institute, we have a clearer picture of the timeline I have to deal with the root causes of this cancer and keep my body from going too far into disease to support me in the future. Because of that, we feel that the next month is the critical stage, where we can either turn this around or the damage to my body will be too much to overcome without even more drastic work. So that means that I am cutting down even more on clients for the next few weeks, asking my city clients to see the other therapists in our clinic whenever they can, and calling or emailing Angie or I directly to get the appointments they need for what only I can deliver, because my online schedule will show not available even though I might be. I don't want to leave any of my clients wanting while I am rebuilding, but I just cannot physically handle the workload for the next few months. If you can, please book with one of our other therapists. If you need me (sacrum work, disk pump, ankle mobilizations, acupressure, energy work) call or email and I or Angie will personally return every message and do my best to fit you in. Thank you so much for the ongoing love and support, and please understand that even in this cutback phase, our spirits and our hopes are high.

Dale - January 28, 2016

Last night we tried a homeopathic (apis mellifica) to control the itch while I'm sleeping, and it worked! I woke up three times and took more, and got at least eight hours of sleep, and did not scratch myself bloody. Yay. Used it all day today to augment the cream, and I'm pretty much itch free.

Emotionally this challenge has been really good for me, as I'm learning very practically how to release each emotion as it comes up. Spiritually, this is the basis of my struggle. I know what I want to do but feel like none of the ways that I've known of doing spirit work are quite right for me at this time. I feel on the precipice of success but like there is still some small piece I am missing. To help that, I am taking every 15 minute chunk of time I have available and doing a little meditation, or a directed healing, or a bit of emotional work. I know that this is the only way that I can change what is happening for me right now.

Heard from Canada Customs in Pennsylvania this AM. They had one question for Angie, and then released the product right away. The only issue is that we won't receive the product until Monday now, but at least we know it is cleared. I'm excited for this.

Angie

Because we live in a rural location, we had the GcMAF delivered to our office in the city. The question that the customs people had for me was "Is this product for re-sale or personal use?". For personal use, was the right answer.

Dale - January 29, 2016

Well, it seems that Apis Mellifica IS the answer to chronic itch. I had another night of at least eight hours total sleep, with two interruptions to eliminate urine and take more of the homeopathic, and I awoke not bleeding from scratching. Throughout the day today I continued to take the Apis whenever I noticed the itch coming back, and I have scratched relatively little today.

I got a call today to confirm that my GI guy wants to schedule a short hospital stay to get an external stent put in to drain the liver of bile. His office, or the office of bed management at U of A hospital, will be calling me Monday to tell me what the schedule is. I see this as a move in the right direction, because I'm still worried about damaging my liver if it can't drain for too long, and this stent (I believe) can be easily removed when the tumour shrinks enough to stop blocking the bile duct.

Today I saw two clients, and I felt better after the second client than I did before the first. It pleases me so much that I can work at a pace that nourishes my spirit and serves my clients. I am still asking all of my clients who can to see one of the other therapists in our clinic, at least half of the time, so that they get what they need and I am not overworked. I have high hopes of being back to full time within months, especially after a day like today where I am able to eat (comfortably) a little more than I ate yesterday. I really think that the protocols that we are using are working to slowly begin to shrink the tumour to manageable size, and we haven't even started with the GcMAF yet.

Dale - January 30, 2016

Physically, I'm doing fine again today. I'm eating more and absorbing more nutrients almost every day. I'm continuing to read two books: "Letting Go" by Dr. David Hawkins and "Emotion and Healing in the Energy Body" by Robert Henderson. It seems more and more that everything I read ends up going in the same direction, the theme of which is to continue to "let go" of old emotional traumas, by identifying them, feeling them, and releasing myself from their hold on me. Considering how much work I've done on this over the years, especially through my acupressure training, I'm amazed at how much more of this I seem to have still to deal with, and how difficult it is to focus on this, in my mind, most important part of my healing journey.

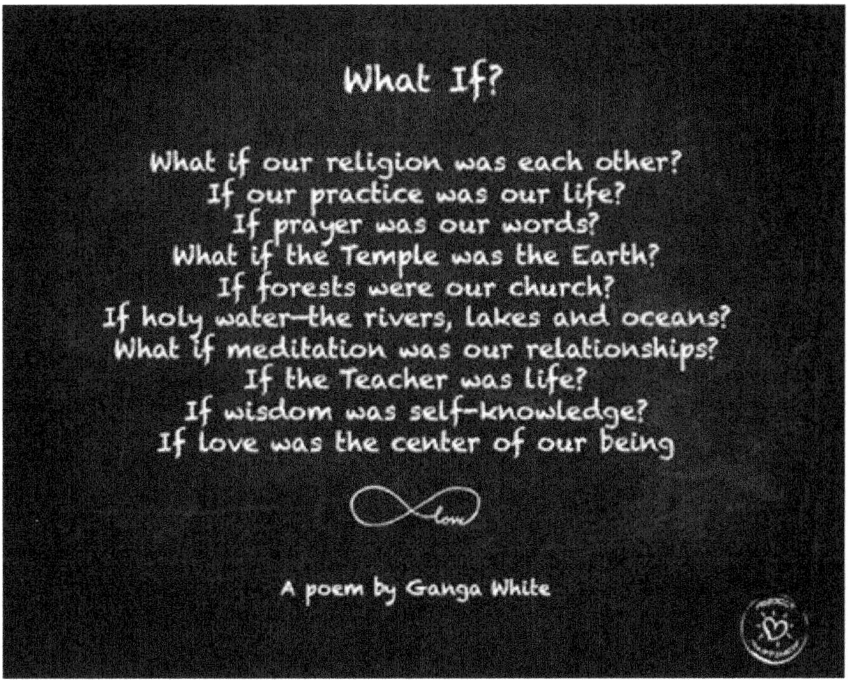
What If?
What if our religion was each other?
If our practice was our life?
If prayer was our words?
What if the Temple was the Earth?
If forests were our church?
If holy water—the rivers, lakes and oceans?
What if meditation was our relationships?
If the Teacher was life?
If wisdom was self-knowledge?
If love was the center of our being
A poem by Ganga White

I want to be clear about something that has come up a few times in the past week. Philosophically and theologically, I believe in Divinity, but I am not a Christian. I know a lot about Christianity because I was a Christian for most of my life, I attended seminary on a path to becoming a minister, I studied religion in university, and I was somewhat of a biblical scholar on the side. I have no problem with other people being Christians, and I wish them peace and joy in their path and gladly accept their prayers for me. I am willing to discuss many aspects of Christianity with friends and clients, and never think of trying to change their minds about their chosen course. The only thing is, it does not fit for me. My biggest problem is with organized religion of almost any faith that I have examined, which demonstrates profoundly that all organized religion is the result of men (and some women) trying to control the masses, and keep people from examining questions that could lead to apostasy.

Dale - January 31, 2016

Well here it is, one month at home, and continuing to improve. I just had a breakfast of home-made sweet potato pancakes, all ingredients designed to nourish my body and not the tumour, and they tasted great! That's partly because Angie prepares everything with love, and partly because it's another new flavor that I can productively consume.

Today was a busy day with visitors and phone calls with family. I love the people who came and called this weekend – each one of them left me feeling stronger, even though I was a bit tired by this evening. I wouldn't trade my friends for any other group – they are all the salt of the earth, and each one of them gave something that no one else could give. Thank you.

I ate a goodly amount today, and got some meditation time and some working on my stuff time. We capped the day off with a supper of Angie's famous Baingan Bartha, a lovely flavorful East Indian recipe that she whips up from scratch. Thank you, baby.

Angie

Cooking is a bit of a passion for me, and Dale was wonderfully easy to please. Being able to create anything at all that he could tolerate now, was a huge success. One of the side effects that people with cancer have to deal with is that the taste buds are affected to the point that many (most) things taste awful. Even their favorite foods are suddenly intolerable. When you're used to cooking for someone who loves pretty much everything it can be frustrating and disheartening when they find it so distasteful. It is an opportunity to remember that taking things personally does not serve us.

Dale - February 1, 2016

Today I had another good day. I'm putting more food in each day than the day before, and I feel that we have stopped the growth of the tumour, and maybe even begun the process of shrinking it, just based on the increased capacity for food and the reduction in itching I noticed today. I saw several clients this morning, and it was wonderful to be able to work with them. Then off to the city to consult with a pain specialist, and we were able to work out a plan to control the pain indefinitely. Back out to the ranch where my 3:30 client stood me up (ouch!), and sadly that took one away from someone who would have appreciated it in this time of reduced availability.

Finally, I received an Access Bars treatment from a good friend this evening, and I'm still absorbing that. Angie got home after 5:00 (while I was receiving my treatment) with the package from The Netherlands, and so we now have the Goleic (GcMAF) in hand. Because of some slight confusion over delivery method, I'm going to wait until tomorrow for the first dose, and I expect nothing but miraculous progress from here on out.

I just want to take this opportunity to tell people one simple thing, which is "if you (or someone you know) get a cancer diagnosis, do not wait for the system to start you on a program to get you healthy again. Take charge of your life, do the research, call me or Dr. Steinke or someone else who has had success with treating cancer, and start doing the things immediately that will support your body so you can take yourself to cancer-free." If I had known a month ago what I know now, I would have started with these protocols January 1 when I got out of the hospital. As it was, it took a couple of weeks to get things rolling, because we did not know what was worth trying.

Dale - February 2, 2016

Have you ever asked yourself "I wonder what I would change if I knew I was dying?" Well, I don't think I'm dying, but at the same time there is a very real possibility that I could in the next months, and that has prompted me to ask that question. So far, the answer is "Not as much as I would have thought two months ago" (before Cody and my diagnosis). The only thing that really changed so far is that I'm a lot more careful about what I put in my body than I ever was. When death is "in the room", everything you put in is important. Why does it take this extreme to get serious about eating to live instead of living to eat?

Got my first dose of Goleic (GcMAF) today, intravenous, care of my naturopath. I don't know if I was expecting to feel something different after one dose, but I am feeling so positive lately that I find myself expecting a shift at any moment. What a wonderful feeling. Continuing to eat like a lumberjack (OK, maybe the child of a lumberjack . . . a very small child of a lumberjack?) and feel like I'm being nourished more and more by what is going in. Dropped a little more and I'm at 148 lbs. now. Soon have to carry rocks in my pockets, especially when the spring winds pick up here. Or, buy less baggy clothes.

They called me today and said drop everything and come to the hospital now so we can do the liver drain tomorrow. I said I need a little warning, my client is already on her way here. They said, the bed won't be available in a couple of hours. I said I'll get back to you, and then I forgot to phone them. I'll have to phone tomorrow morning and apologize, but meanwhile I'm questioning the need for this procedure, based on what I'm feeling. So I need to do a little intentioning around clarity as to whether I need this or not, by morning.

Dale - February 3, 2016

I spent an extremely restless night with the itch in my feet so bad that with itch cream, Apis and everything else I could do I still lost two hours of sleep in the middle of the night. I sat up and read until my feet got chilled (Angie said "blocks of ice") and was finally able to go back to sleep @ 3:30 AM. I woke up at 7:30 feeling groggy but functional and got a call from U of A at 8:00 to say "get down here and we'll do the procedure today". I moved my client today to Friday, showered, slathered in itch cream, hurried to the hospital (speeding ticket on the way in) and arrived to realize: no health care card or photo id. Anyway, whether it was my charming good nature or cadaverous appearance, they let me in.

So, I met my new internist and his two interns today. I found out something that I didn't know, that the tumour has actually infiltrated the duodenum as well as the lungs. When I asked if the procedure was reversible when the tumour shrinks, they looked at me like I was nuts. But they did allow that the procedure is reversible. I guess in their view, me and my "witchdoctor protocols" are hopeless. LOL!

Laying here until 3:00 when they were able to decide they were putting it off until tomorrow. So now I can eat, but nothing they can provide. Good thing Angie thought to pack some Hippocrates Soup and some dried figs and some sparkling mineral water. Hopefully they'll bring something for supper that I can eat.

Angie - February 3, 2016 - posted on Facebook

So, here's the thing. When I lost Cody it was sudden and there wasn't a damn thing I could do about it. This is totally different: I spend every waking hour doing something or thinking about something I CAN DO. Mostly it's trying to keep weight on Dale in a way that does him no harm. He can't digest meat or fats, dairy is out and sugar and carbs are a definite no, no. It's a huge effort and to be honest I feel as though this cancer is consuming me as well as it is Dale. My life is in complete chaos, I have no time to catch up and we're always on the run. That being said, I will gladly do it for as long as it takes. Dale is worth all the effort and I can't imagine my life without him... thankfully I don't really have time to think about that, or my loss of Cody.

So a day like today, where Dale is deprived of all the usual protocols (including the new Goleic) and was not allowed to eat for 21 hours, is pretty hard to take. This was a recurring theme last time Dale was in the U of A, three times they starved him and then cancelled the tests. I know we can't control everything and that "letting go" has great value but quite frankly this was more than a little frustrating and I've got a ways to go before I'm that enlightened.

Dale - February 4, 2016

February 3, 9:30 PM: I'm going to get a hole poked in my liver tomorrow, and the doctor on the ward prescribed me Heparin (a blood thinner) tonight. I don't see how that could possibly be a good combo, but when I said I didn't want it the student nurse-practitioner kinda blew a gasket. Then when my roommate also refused his, she lost it. Very sad situation. (Update Dr. McNally, who did my procedure said it was a very good call on my part).

On another note, Dr. Zepeda came in and chatted with me about this procedure earlier today. I like him a lot, he really acts like he cares and he seems to hear me when I talk. At the shift change today my BP was 94/59, heart rate 49. I really think this weight-loss program is working. I went up and down 8 flights of stairs for exercise, mission successful. 10:50 PM I received an oral medication for the itch: Cholestyramine. It seems to work pretty fast so I'm expecting a good night's sleep. Two old friends called me today and it was really uplifting to re-connect with them. I spent another long day without any liquid or food and expected they'd come to cancel the procedure yet again. To my surprise they came in the room @ 3:00 and said that I was going to be very happy. At 3:20 they took me down to get the liver stent. Before they could do it they had to give me some sugar pills because my blood sugar was at 2.7, that what happens when you don't eat.

I've been reading Dr. David Hawkins book "Letting Go" and so decided to "let go" of what happens today. I had a plan for them doing the procedure and another if they didn't. And then, I completely "let go" of needing it to be one way or the other. Shortly after I got the good news and found out later on that they stayed late to get it done for me. Dr. McNally and his amazing team of nurses, and their great attitudes and their confidence helped me to continue to "let go" of my concern for the outcome. It's two hours later, and I feel great (and it's not just the drugs talking). More on exactly what they did and plan to do in the next few days will follow in tomorrow's post.

Angie

At around 2:00 I had a talk with the nurses in the station about Dale's situation, the fact that he has been starved on several occasions and the importance of him getting the procedure done. I have no idea whether or not I had any impact but I do know that they heard me and they truly seemed to care.

Dale - February 5, 2016

So, here's the scoop on what they did yesterday: they used ultrasound to determine the best place in my liver to place the drain (Dr. McNally let me watch with him and his student – cool), and then they drugged me up pretty good without knocking me out and pushed a wire in between my ribs on the right side, through my liver, and then into the common bile duct and out to the duodenum. Then they placed a stent in the bile duct so that some bile will go into the duodenum, left a hose imbedded to a drain on the outside, and taped me all up, hung a bag on the hose, and sent me back to my room. I heard everything they said until the end of the procedure when they let me go to sleep while they finished everything up, and it sounded very encouraging. When Dr. Zepeda did the original endoscope Dec. 31, he could not get into the bile duct, but he did the next best thing in leaving a stent in the duodenum so that my stomach would be able to release food into the small intestine, and this time they were able to get into the bile duct (albeit from a different angle) and place a stent there easily. I heard the doctor say that there was more space there than he expected, which would mean that the protocols we are following are working to shrink the tumours.

So at the end of the procedure, the plan was to drain all of the excess bile from my liver and the rest of my system, and then to cap the tube and allow the bile to drain into the duodenum. Dr. McNally thinks I'll stay in the hospital for another couple of days, and then he'll look at any adjustments he wants to make and then send me home early next week.

At 5:00 on Feb. 5 the senior intern on my case (Zach – Dr. Zacharia Mansour) came into my room and asked me if I'd be OK going home today. So they taught me how to look after my external bag and apparatus, gave me some supplies that are harder to buy "on the outside" and discharged me about 6:30. Thank you. My opinion of Dr. Mansour and Dr. Gutfreund (senior resident on my case this time) has gone up considerably since my first meeting with them on the third of this month. I believe that they actually heard me, and perhaps were just a little unsettled initially by my attitude (of I AM going to survive this).

Dale - February 6, 2016

So, by the time I left the hospital yesterday, we had drained 1.9 litres of excess bile from my liver. I'm still yellow, and itchy as can be, but it is looking better. I got a little scare this morning when I got a little over 100 ml of blood passing into the bile bag, but after I emptied that, only bile continued to come out. The rate of release has slowed considerably, but I'm keeping the bag on until it gets right down, and then I will remove the bag, cap the tube, and allow the bile to drain only into the duodenum.

The last two days in the hospital, Angie smuggled my "medicine" in, so I only lost one day of treatment to the hospital stay. Angie also brought me food for all my meals in the hospital, as the only things they brought me that I could take in were vegetable broth (I don't want to know what kinds of GMOs and non-organics were in that) and Camomile tea. I do not want to complain, because again, the people at the hospital were all awesome (especially the majority of the nursing staff and including the porters who moved me around for the procedures), but the problem seems to be the sheer massive size of the operation at U of A hospital, and how that size slows communication.

Since this last procedure, I have been very tired, sleeping 8 hours at night and also napping for a few hours during the day. Must be all the healing going on. Speaking of tired, I forgot to mention yesterday that Dr. McNally and his staff stayed past their normal quitting time to do this procedure, and I never got a chance to thank him for that, although I believe I thanked the OR nurses (through my post-op grogginess). They are doing everything that they can to keep up with demand, and I truly appreciate that.

So far since I got home, including the blood from my liver, we have drained another litre of bile and fluids from my liver. No wonder I was so yellow and so itchy. Between my blood, the fatty subcutaneous layer, and my liver, I must have had nearly 4 litres of excess bile in me. Thank you liver and kidneys for supporting me through this. Another thing I learned in this trip to the hospital is that the tumour itself had infiltrated the duodenum. I wish that I had known the right questions to ask so that I would have had the complete picture right from the start. I don't know if they were trying to be gentle or whether they just assumed that I didn't need to know these things, but if I had to do it over I think I would ask more questions from the start. I suspect that there was a little bit of not wanting to appear weak that stopped me from asking lots of questions this time, but I now realize that I needed to have the complete picture earlier so that I could do better visualizations.

Angie

A word about large institutions like U of A hospital, there seemed to be a huge disconnect in the system regarding dietary needs. Dale received a duodenal stent, and there are many restrictions involved with that (we found out a week later, after consulting with Dr. Zepeda on our own) such as bread and dry meats which can become lodged in the stent. After Dale's procedure they brought him a salmon sandwich, it ended up taking several days to move through his system. A large price to pay after being able to finally enjoy something to eat.

Dale - February 7, 2016

Last night I slept eight and a half hours without getting up to urinate, empty my bag, or scratch (Angie was up two hours before me and gave me some Apis Mellifica to make sure I didn't start to itch). That is incredible! Also, after eight and a half hours there was only about 100 ml of lovely golden-brown bile in the bag, whereas up to now I've filled the bag to about 400 ml in six hours or less, and the bile has ranged from the color and texture of used motor oil to darker brown or even a little reddish with the blood. Today I thought I would remove the bag and cap the tube, hopefully for the duration, and just monitor carefully to make sure the bile continues to drain through the stent, but as I was sitting up it drained more rapidly than while I was sleeping, and my urine is still dark, so I still have an excess of bile in my system. I still have to be careful not to eat anything that could potentially block the duodenal stent, but I should be able to start adding fats and maybe even white meat into the diet, and maybe reverse this weight-loss.

Had a lovely visit last night with Jake and Kim, who drove out from Nanaimo. Due to car trouble, Jake and Kim will stay for a few days with us and then make plans to get home once the Jeep is fixed. So we spent a pretty quiet day today.

Angie

A month or so later we noticed what looked like bright red blood passing into the bile bag again, and because we had sometimes noticed brilliant orange carrot juice flowing through, we surmised (after also consulting with the doctor) that rather than blood it was beet juice we were seeing. That was a huge relief!

Dale - February 8, 2016

Today was an interesting day. I woke up feeling hungry, and like I had turned the corner in some ways. Had a good breakfast and initial protocols, saw a few clients (with Kim doing the majority of the massage work and me adding my touch where needed), but have not really been able to eat more since then. Experiencing more epi-gastric pain than usual, but managed to drink another litre of water. Meditation was valuable today, and had some insights into how far I've come in the last two months. Around 6:00, I had the sudden realization that the reason I'm in so much discomfort today is that I haven't had a dose of my medical marijuana for about 27 hours. I don't know how it's possible to completely miss a part of my daily protocol without noticing it, but there you go – it happened. Resolution: pay more attention to the protocols!

Dale - February 9, 2016

Still suffering from something I ate in the hospital, so I've got a mild blockage at the duodenum again, but at least liquids are slowly seeping through. I spent the night sleeping sitting up again, but I got eight hours of sleep without itching, so some things are going in the right direction. Spent a few hours today visiting my nurses on 5C4 (to pick up my iPhone charger I missed while checking out), down at diagnostic imaging buying the videos of all my procedures at the UAH, and having tea. Then off for the weekly blood tests to monitor liver function, pick up a few groceries, stop at Home Depot for a doorknob – a perfectly normal day. Took a last minute client between my vitamin C-IV and the trip to the hospital, and will see one more at 5:15 before I go home. Spent all my spare time today doing visceral manipulation to get the stomach to empty, and visualizations, and I'm finally getting somewhere. Hopefully I will be able to eat tomorrow.

Angie

Dale ate a small piece of cheese that was part of a meal they offered in the hospital. He did not think that such a small thing could cause so much trouble. How often do we all make those kinds of choices, especially around food?

Dale - February 10, 2016

Today I saw one acupressure client in the morning, then worked on some of my protocols and had a long conversation with the homecare co-ordinator from the Cross. Apparently I qualify for some level of homecare and I'm going to accept that so that we can at least be sure that there is no problem with the PCT exit on my ribcage. Then I got a real good massage from Kim where she was able to work out a few things for me, and spent the rest of the day working on my "stuff".

Dale - February 11, 2016

Yesterday was a very strange day, as I've been able to eat and drink so much more than I have for the last week, and I feel quite a bit stronger and more hopeful than I did the day before. It is amazing how much harder it is to maintain a positive outlook when your body won't seem to accept any nourishment for days on end and it begins to feel like this is a challenge that I'm not equipped to deal with. And I want to make it perfectly clear that this is not an issue of appetite. I have been quite hungry through this whole thing, it is just that my stomach has been feeling so full that I have not been able to put any food in, and what little I have been able to put in has tasted "weird". I really feel that as much as I appreciate the staff at the hospital, I need to avoid staying there as much as I can. So yesterday was a day of transition for me, from "can't" to "will".

One of the other positive side effects of the new stent is that the itching has steadily gotten better. Wednesday and yesterday, I did not have to use the itch creams or the antihistamines. A few applications of Apis Mellifica were all that I required yesterday, and today I'm thinking I may not even need that. That is a bonus, but something else interesting has come up. I have a pain in the liver area that feels much like it did when they were pushing the probe through during the insert of the PCT. Now I remember saying I would take the pain back to relieve the itching, and I hope this is not my deal because I don't know that I'm really willing to accept that level of pain as a trade-off! I will monitor this through the day, and see what comes of it and what other adjustments I may have to make, and hope this is just another phase I am moving through.

Dale - February 12, 2016

Well here it is evening, and I feel like I just had constant pain all day today. I did my regular routine this morning, took all of the supplements related to pain that I normally take, had a nice light day work-wise, so really not sure where this is coming from. The pain feels centred in the liver, in the front of the liver right about where the probe goes out to the common bile duct, and I have only had moments of relief all day, combined with acid reflux which hasn't been a problem since December. Tomorrow the homecare nurse is coming, so we will see if she notices anything that Angie and I have missed. On other fronts, nothing new to report.

Dale - February 13, 2016

This morning started off with an unexpected surprise – I woke up with very little pain. After the way my day ended yesterday, I was thinking I might have to go to emergency again today, just to figure out where all the pain was coming from. I keep expecting it to hurt when I move, and I move into the range of motion where there was pain yesterday, and it just doesn't show up. I'm not complaining, but I really have a hard time believing that the pain is just not there. (Late evening note: a little bit of the pain is back under certain movements, but really nothing in the grand scheme of things. Thank you.)

Well, we had our visit with the homecare nurse, and it turns out she's practically a neighbour of ours. She was extremely helpful, and a pleasant surprise, as I've never had this type of situation before and didn't know what to expect. She was able to reassure us on several points, and really didn't find anything we were doing that needed major change, so that was a comfort too. Angie and I were both quite joyful to find that she was supportive of us "where we were", because as most of you know, we are going out on a bit of a limb with our choices for treatment. Anyway, she was able to restock our supplies, change the under-bandage that holds the hose in place where it exits my body, and confirm that everything is "looking great".

Today was a good day overall, some progress on the spiritual and emotional sides of things, and a better day for nourishment than yesterday. Tomorrow Jim is coming out to change our water filter for us (a business that Jim and I were in together in the 80's) and Linda, Wilf and Mom will also visit for the afternoon and early evening. I am blessed to have the friends and family that I have, and especially blessed to have Angie in my life: not only has she been my rock throughout this challenge, giving me a safe place to anchor myself and freeing me to continue to work on the things that matter, but Angie has completed me over the last ten years in ways that I never thought could be possible for me. I love you, baby.

Angie

And blessed we were, before this happened not many days went by that I wasn't grateful for the life we shared. Even in this horror show I often found things to be grateful for, it's really all about perspective and what you choose to focus on. When we married in 2014 we called it a "Celebration of Love" and we declared "We Choose Love".

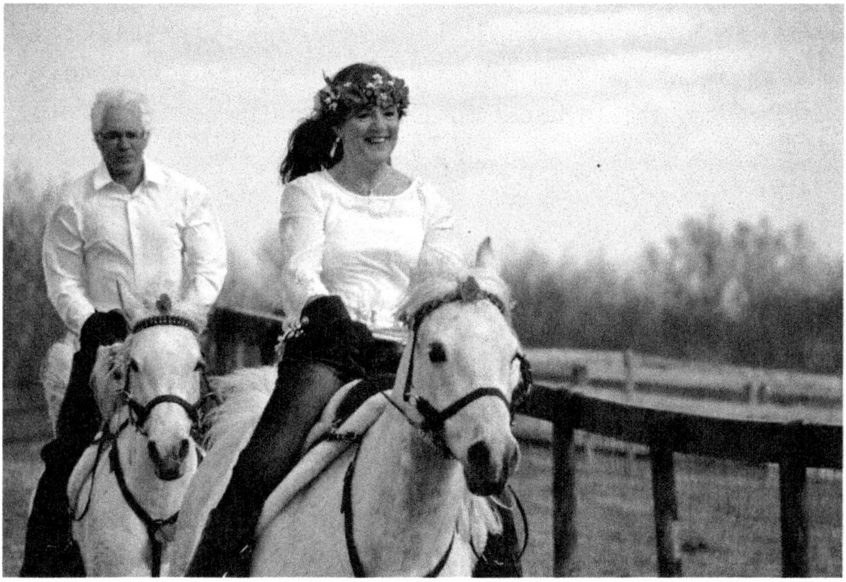

Angie and Dale chose to make their wedding on May 10, 2014, a memorable occasion. They presented themselves to their wedding guests at a full gallop.

Dale - February 14, 2016

Yesterday started out better than the day before, and my morning things all went well. Family showed up, and we had some fun playing card games, just like old times. By early afternoon, however, I was feeling signs of blockage, and by late afternoon it was bad enough that I had to stretch out to relieve it. I was able to put some water in, but really not much else for the rest of the day. Then at supper, I was able to eat 3 spoons of mashed potatoes with gravy. That was a taste that was almost indescribable in its intensity and delight (look at me liking mashed potatoes!).

Unfortunately I was not up to writing my blog last night, but I do feel better again this morning, so hopefully we'll make a bit of progress today. I'm back on the Goleic today after the weekend off, and this is the week we have to decide if I stay on it or not, so I hope we see some definitive improvement in the next few days so that there will be no question.

Dale - February 15, 2016

Today started out with me cancelling my one client, as I was just too tired and weak feeling to do a treatment. I guess yesterday was harder on me than I thought, but I found out with my enema this morning that nothing had passed through my small intestine in the last 24 hours. No wonder I'm down to 139 lbs.! I thought we were doing OK yesterday for the most part, but I'm starting to think I'm not quite as in tune with what's going on in my body as I would like to think.

Today became a day to focus on the protocols that are seeming to work, and leave out the ones that require more effort on my part and may not be having such a positive effect. We figured out that I have to have my oral Vitamin C completely separate from everything else, because its flavor is just so overpowering and I am having a hard time forcing things down that have "weird" flavors. To that effect, I am also stopping the apricot seeds (vitamin B17) because even ground up and mixed with yogurt and stevia, the effort to push them in is just too great for the potential benefit.

Also today, I focused more on meditations, and even found a guided Reiki meditation from William Rand that really spoke to my soul and felt really good to add in today. I feel like I'm finally making progress on the several past-life issues that are tied into this challenge, and it felt like there was another large shift in the energies around this whole situation today. I am surprised at how much Reiki has figured into my journey these days, as I've never really felt called to focus so much on Reiki over the past ten years. Help from Chris, Carol and Cheryl in this regard has seemed to bring new focus into the ways that Reiki can help me, and I thank you ladies sincerely.

Finally, the pain has been much more manageable today, and I feel that all that has gone on has purpose and direction, so how can I not be satisfied? Also, a big thank you to my family for getting the old, worn-out water system replaced with a nice functional efficient system. Jim, you still do good work. I'm impressed, and Mom, thank you. Thanks to Linda and Wilf for being here for me yesterday, even though I wasn't such great company, and thanks to Laura for the phone call this morning. I heard the emotion in your voice, and I appreciate your concern.

Angie

Because Dale was taking the Goleic supplement he had to cut down from 45,000 units IV of vitamin C to 25,000. Dr. Steinke provided us with an oral supplement for the days between IVs. I later began stuffing the ground up apricot seeds into gel capsules so that Dale would not have to taste them.

Dale - February 16, 2016

Today I had my first bowel movement this year without an enema. That was momentous (although it wasn't much of a movement) because it means that stuff was moving out of my stomach and through my small intestine yesterday. After the day I had on Sunday, I was pretty sure that the blockage was the worst it had been since Dec. 28, so this movement today was very encouraging. I attribute a lot of this latest improvement to the self-Reiki on top of the earlier Reiki sessions from my friends.

And now, on another song altogether, today has been a day of huge physical movement. The gurgling and churning from the stomach area has been going on non-stop for hours now (12:45 PM) and things are really moving for me. Now it's late evening, and I've eaten more today than I've eaten in a day since mid-December. I have a little indigestion, but it is manageable. I am excited to see what comes up in the next several days. Had a visit tonight from Shawn and Amy and their girls, it's always interesting when Kylie comes over, and quite raises my spirits.

Dale - February 17, 2016

I had such a good day yesterday, and yet I ended the day with a little pain, I think just from eating too much. I positioned myself carefully for sleep (slightly raised head) and was amazed to get a little better than eight hours. Woke up feeling good and for the third day in a row was able to eat what almost feels like enough. My stomach capacity has increased incredibly in the last few days, and that also tells me that something is changing for the better. I still have a ways to go, but I am so pleased with where I am. As well as the things I am putting into my body, I am doing a lot of energy work on the deeper associations with this form of cancer, and I believe that it is only through the combination of physical and energetic/spiritual work that we are starting to see the signs of a major turnaround.

Angie

As you may have noticed, every day is not like the other. When people asked me how things were going I always referred to it as a roller-coaster ride... up and down and round and round and lots of screaming (silently in my head).

Dale - February 19, 2016

Please note, if I don't post every day, it's not because things are bad. Some days I'm just too tired to write a post, even though I've had a day that is full of marvelousnousity. Nine and one half hours of sleep last night, and waking up feeling hungry! That's four days in a row of improvement now, and I can tell you that is encouraging. The only down side today is that I took the Vitamin C this morning before my smoothie (first time in at least three days), and I have been feeling crappy ever since. I did manage to get my smoothie down (finally), but I am not having a good day pain wise (may also have something to do with skipping my dose last night).

Yesterday was an amazing day, and in spite of the high level of discomfort all day today, I feel like today is a continuation of a series of very positive days. Yesterday Angie and I had a session with a very connected healer in our circle of friends. I asked her to do something new and unusual, and she responded by listening to her guides and angels, and bringing a healing that was deeply shifting for me. It all started with Angie and I both noticing how strongly we react to certain people and their way of speaking/interacting with us. Through meditation and discussion, we both came to the conclusion that this was an opportunity to heal a past-life trauma that we were all involved in, and that is what proceeded to happen. In the process, I was able to come to a new way of thinking about people that cause, or try to cause, harm to us. I am again amazed that most of my profound healings in these past few months have come through my connection to Reiki, which I have often thought of over the last 8 – 10 years as one of my "lesser talents". This gives me reason to re-evaluate my connection to Reiki.

Tonight we will have a couple of friends over for dinner, and then we will all go to Camrose to see one of our favorite performers – Royal Wood at the Augustana campus Performing Arts Centre. I also hope to see several other friends who have said they are also going to the performance.

Not Published on Facebook:

I'm also struggling for the last few days with a feeling of violation, and that tells me something about my attitude towards certain Christians (my sister) and their devotion to something that I have not been able to accept throughout my life, even though I feel I have given it every chance possible. Sadly, after experiencing this belief system in my own life, as I grew up in and tried to live in a strong Christian belief system, I understand where this comes from. Christians are taught to believe that the only purpose they have on earth is to worship God (in whatever form their sect of Christianity accepts) and witness to the lost (everybody else). What many Christians don't understand, my sister included, is that your devotion to your religion becomes offensive when it extends to invalidating the life experiences and spiritual accomplishments of other people (me). I believe that my sister and others like them operate from the very best of intentions, and in some ways that makes it even harder to object to their actions. However, let me make this perfectly clear: I will not try to change your spiritual understanding by argument or force of reason at any time, because that would be the height of arrogance from me. I would appreciate it if others respect my spirituality in the same way.

The result of this feeling of violation was that Angie and I both realized that there was a past life experience that we had to heal. As soon as I realized that, I knew I had to call on Chris E. to facilitate that, and I also knew that she had never done anything like that before, so I called her, and asked her if she would do it and she said yes. After she released her doubts about her ability to do this, it became clear to her what she needed to do, and Angie and she set the time and place. In the session, it was revealed that Chris and I were mid-late teenage friends who joined the Knights Templar during the last days of that organization, and that Angie was a young lady of the same class, and that her and I were lovers. When Chris and I disappeared (presumably murdered with the rest of the Knights Templar). Angie was heartbroken and spent lots of time riding around and looking for me, eventually married, and became a healer.

What came from this for me is that I have an awareness that I can forgive someone who hurts me out of fear, when I am aware that fear is their motivator, yet I am not so quick to forgive someone who hurts me out of greed. What is greed? Merely a fear of 'not having enough'. In fact, if I look at any of the so-called negative emotions, they all have a basis in fear. What if I just assume that if anyone hurts me, they are operating from a base of fear? Then I'd have to forgive all hurts! Oh, MY, to become truly unoffendable!

Dale - February 20, 2016

Again, today was a good day. I had a little difficulty yesterday that we believed was caused by the 10,000 mg Vitamin C oral, so today we tried a different tack: I will attempt four - 2,500 mg doses spread throughout the day. If that works, we will continue at 10,000 daily when I don't get the IV, and if it doesn't work, we will try to figure something else out. So far today I have taken two of the smaller doses and though they were harsh, I seem to be managing ok.

As Angie said (on Facebook), Royal Wood was really good last night, and we all enjoyed the evening. Thank you to Larry for driving, and to Larry and Doreen for their company. I also got to see a few people at the concert that I know from Camrose, and that was quite a treat, even though I feel like I wasn't totally present due to the pain from the stomach and the resulting medication.

Dale - February 21 and 22, 2016

Angie and I want to take a moment again and thank everyone who has been so kind as we focus on getting me well. Neither one of us has been particularly good at asking for help, and sometimes it has been hard for us to accept help, but that has been one of the lessons we have both had to learn in this journey: there are a lot of incredible heart people out there, and a lot of our friends and even acquaintances, fall into that category. As we move forward into a new way of being in this world, we are clearly seeing who is willing to work with us, who appreciates what we have to offer the world, and who does not.

Yesterday, Angie and I both started to work through our course on opening our Akashic Records (Akashic Records Level 1 from Ernesto Ortiz). I am quite excited about the potential here for growth and expansion of my connection to the work that we do, and the potential doors that this will open.

Finally, the nuts and bolts report. I'm feeling pretty good, getting food in still much better than it has been, and feeling like we're still going in the right direction. Today, Dr. Gutfreund called and talked to Angie about my progress. He is the GI specialist who was my doctor my last visit to UA Hospital, when they put in the liver drain, and he wanted to follow up because he wasn't getting the blood work reports to let him know that my bilirubin was getting lower in the bloodstream. He suggested that we might want radiology to assess what is happening with the stent and drain, in case something needs to be moved so that I can eat better, so we should hear something in the next day or so about that. If I don't hear from them by Monday morning, I'll see Dr. Hackett in the afternoon and see if he can order that test in a timely manner – I really don't want to go back to the hospital, even for one night.

Dale - February 23, 2016

Another positive day overall, and some potential good news. This morning, Dr. Gutfreund called to follow up on the bilirubin issue. In my blood, as of Monday afternoon, it was down to just under half of the level when I was discharged Feb. 5. Good enough for us to see skin coloration improvements and for the itching to be completely gone, but not as good as the medical team had expected. So here's the new plan: it's back to the hospital before 8:00 tomorrow morning for blood work, then at 10:00 a cholangiogram, and then possible corrections to the stents. Best news? I expect to be home in my own bed tonight and tomorrow night! Maybe after this, I'll be able to eat a little better.

Angie and I will work a little further tonight on the Akashic Records program, and then try to get to bed a little earlier than usual, so we can get up early enough tomorrow morning to get through my protocols and still get out of here by 6:45 to get to the lab by 8:00 AM. I thank God and all that is Divine every day that I have the partner that I have. She supports me, challenges me, kicks me in the butt, kisses me better, and gives me hope all while being very real, every day and in every circumstance.

Dale - February 24 and 25, 2016

Well. Yesterday was a day, and that's for sure. Angie and I both woke up at 2:00 AM, and neither could get back to sleep. We did some stuff to try to at least get some rest for a few hours, but then at 4:20 AM we had (special home-made) ice cream. Yum. Back to the city for blood draw before 8:00 AM, then over to U of A Hospital for a cholangiogram and possible stent replacement. We checked into the hospital at about 8:30 and then had to wait nearly 2 hours for the correct antibiotic to be brought over, and finally went over for the test at 1:00 PM. In the meantime, they brought me a series of 4 heated blankets to keep me warm – I WANT one of those blanket heaters. Dr. McNally asked me a few questions, and then made the plan as to what they would do. The OR nurses, and Dr. McNally, were incredibly great, they almost made it feel like a day at the spa. Then the bad news. My BP was 90/50, with a heart rate of 45, with O2 sats sitting at 100 (while I was waiting, I had been meditating) and they were afraid to give me any anesthetic because of that, so they elected to do the procedure without anesthetic.

Now, I've always said that pain was merely the interpretation by the brain of a neurological signal, and therefore is not real, but really? They put in the dye, and let me watch on the screen while they identified the situation, and decided to push in a stent that was 4" longer and more than 25% bigger in diameter, to get a better drain and also to put the bile farther down the duodenum, past the partial blockage. As Dr. McNally started to push the new stent, I just kept noticing the pain and releasing it, or reinterpreting it, until he was done. Afterwards the nurses all came up and seemed quite impressed that my heart rate and BP did not change at all throughout the procedure. One nurse even called me a ninja, and another said she'd never seen anyone do that in all her time in that department, which helped me to feel pretty good about what I had learned to do.

Then back to the recovery room at 3:00, where Angie was waiting for me, and because there was no anesthetic in my system, I only had to wait three hours under observation before they could release me, so at 6:00 PM after a nice little nap under another heated blanket they kicked me out. Maybe because I went to sleep for a bit I had the hardest time getting warm, and the pain was quite a bit worse after the nap than it had been during the procedure, but we were able to deal with it. Home and to bed by 9:00 PM, and I slept through until 8:00 AM this morning, and I feel a lot better this AM. Angie said I groaned and grunted a lot while I was sleeping, and I do remember quite a lot of pain at times while lying in bed when I was awake, but now I can breathe without big pain, although I'm still a little leery of sneezing or coughing.

I am so grateful to my body for staying healthy in every other way during this challenge. I have not gotten a cold or the flu while I've been dealing with this challenge, and that is just amazing to me. The fact that Angie has also maintained her health during this time is also amazing, only because her stress levels are as high as I've ever seen them, so overall I'd say that our lifestyle and belief systems are both being validated by what is happening. Yet another of the many blessings we continue to receive on a daily basis. Finally, one last note: I mentioned the OR nurses, who I think are rock stars, but I don't want to forget the nurses and other staff in the recovery room. Their positive attitudes and attention to their patients were absolutely spot on. Not just towards me, but I got to watch them interact with the other dozen or so patients in the recovery room and these are definitely the under sung heroes of UAH.

Angie

At this point in time Dale was starting to include some of the responses that he received on Facebook in the document he had created about his journey.

Patti B. - This is a comment on Angie's post about being unoffendable. Just wanted to say this is one of the hardest things for me to do. A pretty common response I have to other people's behaviour is to feel hurt. To let go of that hurt and move on is killer hard for me. The Pentecostal in me wants them to be judged and punished. I feel like I'm making progress on this.

Angie

I think the post that Patti is referring to was from Wayne Dyer: "Every moment that you spend upset, despaired, anguished, angry or hurt because of the behaviour of anybody else in your life is a moment in which you've given up control of your life".

Dale - Oh, Patti, I know exactly what you mean. I have been practicing at this (and Angie, too) since we got together in 2007, and we have times still where we fail (especially while driving - a gift from my father) but overall, it gets better (not necessarily easier) as time and practice accumulates. I will also tell you that being in my circumstance puts a slightly different perspective on the whole question. The thing I would like to say to you is first, congratulations for even trying. That is awesome.

And secondly, there is no substitute for staying present, even in the failures, because you will learn something at each attempt.

Dale - February 26, 2016

Just so you all know, I want to confess that I am not a rock. I am human, and sometimes that means that I go to "the dark place" (and not just when I'm reading Stephen King, the world's greatest living author). Dying doesn't scare me (there are times when I would almost welcome death) but what does scare me is what happens to Angie if I pass in the next little while. The stress of watching her stress over how I'm not able to eat, and seeing how consumed she is with MY stuff, finally hit a boiling point yesterday, and we had a mutual melt-down that actually proved to be quite cathartic in the end, as a lot of things that needed to be said, and hadn't been said, came out. The last time I was in the hospital for a liver stent it took me almost a week to recuperate, and I guess I had forgotten that as I was in so much pain Wednesday night and all day yesterday that, until Angie reminded me, I was starting to believe that I was in big trouble. The pain is better today, and I am trying to put in better nutrition, and I am starting to feel like I am actually improving. So yes, even the strong have their weak moments, and I think that is what lets us know that we are strong – we recover from those moments, and go on.

Home care dropped in yesterday with some more supplies so we won't run out of anything before she comes next week to supervise Angie changing my bandage where the bile line exits my abdomen. I am both surprised and impressed with the service that is being provided – I had no idea that this was even a possibility, and yet this is one of the more compassionate uses of health care spending that I have seen. Thank you Lauren, and Alberta Health Care.

We heard yesterday that I may be able to apply for a CPP disability pension, and so we will explore that next week. I had not thought about that possibility, either, so if it IS possible, that will be a welcome aid, and might at least help get us through this dark patch, financially.

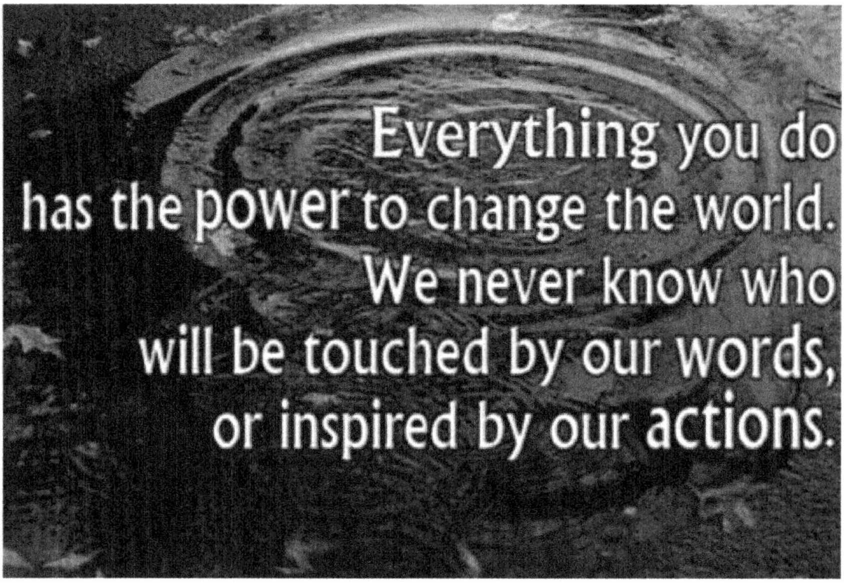
Everything you do
has the power to change the world.
We never know who
will be touched by our words,
or inspired by our actions.

Angie

By this point in time Dale and I had decided that the account of his journey should be available as a book. The positive response to his posts was mindboggling. One of the main reasons I saw fit to go back through the document and add my thoughts and feelings was because I did not often post about them. And, I do believe there is value for those interested in our journey to know the "other side". I knew that Dale worried about me, too much I believed, and while I did release the emotions that were seething inside (you can cry pretty hard when the Vitamix is running on high!) I did not often release them in front of Dale. Don't get me wrong, I was always real with Dale, I did not pretend that everything was alright because it most certainly was not. I did however choose to be somewhat discreet while still wearing my heart on my sleeve.

February 27, 2016

I forgot to mention that on Thursday Dell, a friend of ours who has been through a very similar journey herself, and is quite familiar with what we are going through, donated a queen sized mattress heater with dual controls when she heard about how cold I am so often now (the story of the hot blankets in the hospital). She also offered the benefit of her wisdom gleaned through having been through this and her support in other ways. Thank you, Dell, you are truly one of the people we want to stay connected to.

Yesterday was a strange day in some ways, because I was still feeling a lot of pain from the procedure on Wednesday, and even though I felt I was improving, I just could not face seeing three clients. I moved one to next week (thank you, Christine), one cancelled because she got called out of town, and I ended up seeing one client which was just perfect. I had the time to work on my stuff and do some reading and some writing, which is all very important to me, and for that I thank my friends, clients, and the Universe. Yesterday evening, Angie and I drove into town to have supper at Syphay on Calgary Trail with Samantha, Kim, Karon, Michele, Fraezor and Ashtara. I am so glad that we did, as the energy at that table, with 8 people of like mind, was very healing and calming. I ate all the broth from a large Wonton Soup, and shared a mango ice cream with Angie, while we talked about all manner of things, without spending the two hours focused on solely "my illness". Also, Michele had some interesting facts to share about another version of the GcMAF that were both encouraging and also exciting, and several people had some suggestions for ways of implementing our future clinic ideas. And by the way, if you want a taste treat in an unpretentious location, and you like Thai food, either of the Syphay locations have proven to be exceptional.

This morning I woke up after a mere eight hours of sleep and I feel the best I have felt in some time. It is quite surprising how just feeling better after a period of not can change my whole attitude. Today will be a day of reading, meditating, writing, and possibly ending with a visit from Dennis and Mary-Lynn. I (and I know Angie as well) am looking forward to a quiet weekend and maybe even a little horsey time (probably grooming, not likely riding with this liver stent in place).

Dale - February 28, 2016

Yesterday was a really good day again. I didn't eat the most I've eaten since this began, but I did eat quite a bit, and probably the most I've eaten since the liver stent was first put in on February 4. Dennis is still suffering from a cold, and they decided not to come this weekend after all, so we had the whole day to ourselves. I talked to my friend Larry and he is suffering a bit but recuperating from his operation and I am so glad.

I looked up some things in my copy of Deadman's (the Bible on acupoints) and found some very useful things to try. I normally think systemically on acupoints, looking for big patterns and Strange Flow treatments, and until Samantha reminded me on Friday night I had completely neglected to use the reference section of Deadman for my situation, so needless to say I was pleasantly surprised to find some things that were very helpful and using only a few points in combinations I don't normally use. This will be something I can apply to future clients, another gift to me from this situation I'm in.

This morning, Angie figured out how many calories are in a glass of carrot (and etc.) juice, and I decided that I will not drink water anymore until I have had my five glasses of juice each day. Those five glasses plus the smoothie put me over 1500 calories, so if I can get those in plus a little more nourishment, I may be able to start putting some weight back on. Hallelujah! The other thing I discovered yesterday is that the ester-C 1000 mg tablets (horse pills) can all go in if I spread them out over the day, so I can start getting 10,000 mg of C daily again with so far, no problems.

Another thing that happened today is that during my Akashic meditation I felt like I needed to place a piece of black tourmaline crystal over the tumour, and it felt like some dark energy was being pulled out of my pancreas area into the crystal. We did a little research on the crystal, and it makes some sense, so I will continue to use the crystals I have and listen to my intuition on this.

Finally, thank you so much to all of our friends who have been so kind and supportive over the past weeks and months. If you've messaged me and I haven't responded right away, please know that I appreciate you, but I am conserving my resources and so may put off a response when I'm feeling a bit overwhelmed. Some days I just get too many messages to respond to them all that day, but I sincerely appreciate your interest and will always try to respond in some manner.

Angie

As Dale mentions the tumour I am reminded of my thoughts, and sometimes brief conversations with the thing. I told it how silly it was for creating a situation where its growth would also cause its demise, after all it could not survive without its host. In all of this I also began to view the body as an organism, one that has survival instincts and a myriad of functions all depending on one another for survival. I think it also helped me to think of it this way because I could somehow separate the true essence of Dale from his body which made it a bit easier to cope.

Dale - February 29, 2016

Today I feel mysteriously full, and the nourishment is just not going in like it did yesterday. I am truly mystified by this, as I feel that there is no reason for this feeling, and yet when I try to put nourishment in in spite of the feeling, I am rewarded with pain and discomfort that seems to have no logical cause. So today I will focus on getting in the five juices, the ten horse capsules, and the Goleic, and if anything else goes in that will be a bonus.

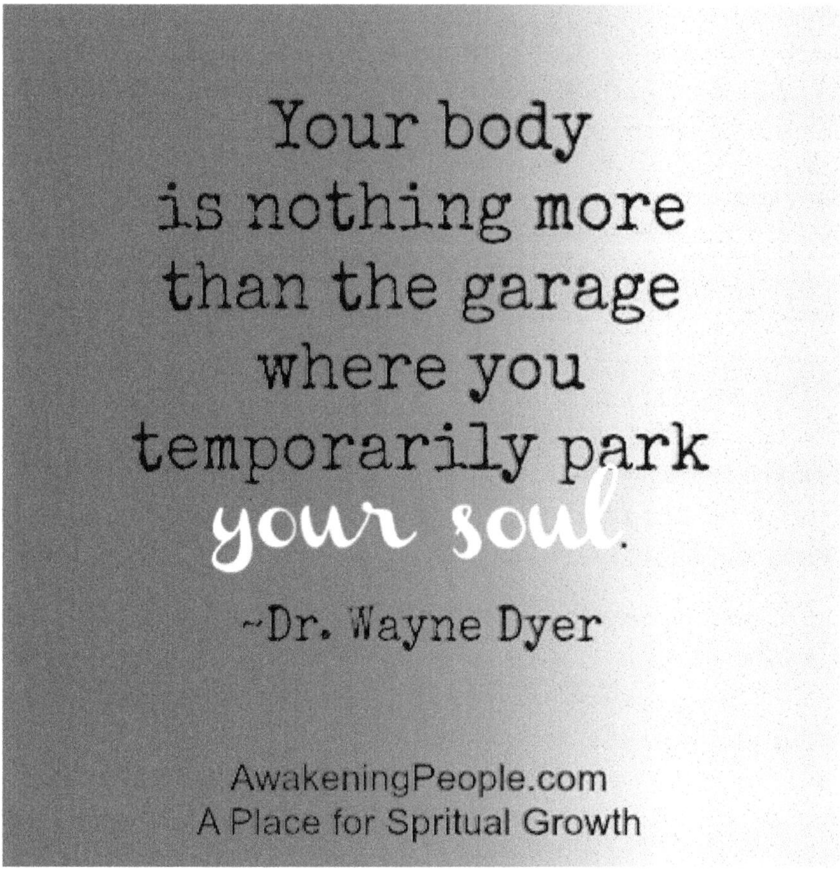
Your body
is nothing more
than the garage
where you
temporarily park
your soul.
~Dr. Wayne Dyer
AwakeningPeople.com
A Place for Spritual Growth

In *"The Toltec Art of Life and Death"* by *Don Miguel Ruiz,* I read something interesting today. He says on pp. 122,123:

"I watch humanity suffer in the name of love, and I attempt to deliver a better message. I encourage people to love themselves. I show them how respect can open doors, while fear only closes them. *Respect rules heaven, and heaven is within our grasp with every choice we make. No one should have to earn respect. We are reflections of life itself. We can respect one another for existing; and we can respect other dreams, no matter how they may differ from our own. Many interpretations of reality exist, and they have a right to exist. We can say yes to someone or we can say no, but* we defeat ourselves when we deny someone simple respect." (bolding is mine, not the author's).

My thoughts in regards to Christians: By other dreams, he means other ways of seeing the world. That is about you and me - we see the world differently. If you read this quote carefully, it will explain how I see the world, not exactly like he does, but very closely. So, I respect your dream, and wish you joy, satisfaction and fulfillment in it. I would hope that you can respect my dream, though I'm sure you don't understand my movement from the boy and young man who believed like you do to the mature man with a completely different view. Remember, I studied church history, and the history of Christianity, and I know where many of the injustices and mistakes in the bible come from. You may not have studied these things, because you accept a lot on faith, including faith in your teachers.

One of my clients today is on an interesting journey, and it warms my soul every time I see her because she is so engaged in her journey. It is entirely one thing to be mindfully engaged, but shifting that to heartful engagement takes the progress out of the realm of accumulation of knowledge (which is NOT truth, but often an easier substitute for truth) and places the path squarely in line with accumulation of wisdom. It does my heart good to see someone coming into their own as a healer, especially a healer of life, and potentially then a healer of Earth.

Dale - March 1, 2016

One of the benefits of going through hard times is that it will become quite apparent who will be your tribe, and who will not. At the Enerchi Massage clinic, we had some people who turned out not to be part of our tribe, and they have all left us in the month of February. I wish them well in their futures, and hope that their futures give them all the success that they deserve. They wouldn't have been with us in the first place if we didn't believe in them, but now it is time to create a new vision of our clinic, and possibly a new direction. We have the space and the presence, so that is the beginning. Some of our associates do believe in us, however, and with their help we will remain open and on the road to that new vision.

Former co-worker - Dale, everyone at Enerchi wanted to be a part of your tribe. Everyone tried very hard. At the end of the day, we all have our family to take care of and it had nothing to do with you. At the end of the day, we all need a roof on our head and food to eat. And we might have a family that depends on that. Don't take it personally. It has absolutely nothing to do with you, it has everything to do with livelihood. Do not discredit those people that have stayed and tried. Because believe it or not, they have. And they love you. But like I said, we also have a family to take care of.

Another former co-worker - The last 2 months have been a struggle on an emotional level regarding dual relationships. As a business owner I needed to look after my business, so that I could feed my family, pay bills etc. As a friend and colleague I wanted to stay and show my support, believing that everything would work out for the best in terms of the situation at hand. I made the decision to move forward to take care of my family and business instead. Perhaps things could have been dealt differently, better communication between both sides, meeting with all that were affected, and maybe work together to figure out how to move forward from this. I am hurt that my decision has given people a sense of abandonment and lack of support. However I will continue to support the journey this person is on right now, and if anyone can beat it he can. Overall though I am grateful for taking the opportunity that presented itself to me and am excited to see what the future brings.

Today I feel a little stronger again physically, but the day did not start out that way. I was quite uncomfortable when I went to bed last night, but got three hours of sleep before the monkey brain kicked in, and I sat up reading from 1:00 AM until 6:30 when it was time to get up. I was in some mild distress through my morning routine, but had a 90 minute nap with my IV this morning, and started feeling better after the IV and treatment from Dr. Steinke. I've been able to drink my morning smoothie and a second juice, so am getting back on track for calories.

Today a friend came over and cleaned our house while we were away. That was such an awesome thing to do, and I thank you from the bottom of my heart, as I know

Angie does too. On another positive note, I'm up a few pounds and was at 137 this morning. Needs a little work yet, but it is the right direction for a change.

Angie

Many months later I still find myself struggling with the way I feel about what happened with our business. It's very difficult to predict how people will handle a situation like this. We found ourselves being astonished at how many people, that we would never have expected, offered and gave support in amazing ways. And our co-workers, whom we had great respect for, were unable to speak to us about what they were feeling and chose instead to send us an email to say they were leaving our company. People make choices based on their perspectives and I do my best to respect that. I expected more from them and that is my mistake, which is why I continue to struggle. We went through a rough patch after this and had to do a lot of processing to come to terms with it. We cannot change another's perspective but we can change ours and that is what can ease our suffering.

It is also interesting to note that many people had, and still have, no idea how to relate to us. I can only speculate that they are afraid to "say the wrong thing", or "become emotional" or just plain "don't want to face it". We never know what others base their actions on and it is our expectations and speculations that create our own pain.

This whole idea of letting go of the need to analyze why others do what they do, based on our expectations, is challenging. One might think that it would be easier to let go when it involves someone who is close to us but I believe that sometimes that's even harder. If our partner behaves in a manner that is not what we anticipate, how much time and energy is often spent in trying to figure out why they did not act differently. And what about the time and energy we spend trying to "fix" them, or make them understand how they let us down. Of course there are circumstances where we can justify our dismay with other people's actions, for instance when physical violence is involved but even then we cannot change the other person, we can only attempt to understand our own reaction and motivations around the circumstances.

Believe it or not, neither Dale nor I are perfect people LOL! We had to work very hard to have the relationship that we did. When either of us found ourselves being "triggered" we had to consciously put our efforts into figuring out what it was in OURSELVES that brought out the intense and uncomfortable emotions rather than blaming the other person for "pushing the button". Having a great relationship is hard work.

Dale - March 2 and 3, 2016

This is shaping up to be a good week for us, although it has not been an easy week. Angie and I both have been through some very emotionally wringing times, as we have experienced some of the most intense highs and lows we have felt since the day of the diagnosis, all in a matter of a few days. We both agreed that, in fact, this week has been more emotionally draining than the actual diagnosis itself was. Because we are so connected, we feel each others' often unspoken pain, and then we find ourselves trying to protect each other from that pain by holding it in and hiding it, until, like a pressure cooker, the steam just has to come out because there is no place left to store it. Thankfully, we understand each other well enough now that we do not allow these releases to poison our relationship, and every time this has happened we grow closer and stronger instead of apart, as we are able to see the motivation behind what is happening and process the pain a little more each time. This is Love in action, and a reflection of the vows Angie and I wrote for our wedding:

We have not fallen in love but rather risen in love. For this, I will be grateful every day.
I can't help but believe that I have been here before by your side, more than once.
I promise to continue to support you and encourage you to thrive and grow and become all you can be. In becoming one we remain free to be stronger individuals.
I promise to be real with you, and honest with you, even when it's hard. You are perfect, just as you are.
I realize that I am responsible for the way I feel.
With you I am empowered to choose what lifts me up

I choose LOVE

An unexpected stress this week has been our struggle to understand and accept the changes that have occurred at our Edmonton clinic in the last weeks. While it is easy to say that we understand the need for other people to look after themselves, it is still hard to deal with the emotions that arise when other people do things in a way that is different than what we would do or what we would hope for, especially when we are experiencing so many other emotional trials. This has been a very real and visceral lesson in letting go of putting an interpretation on other people's actions based on "what I would do", and I hope that all the people involved understand that both parties need to absorb these lessons for their own growth and progress.

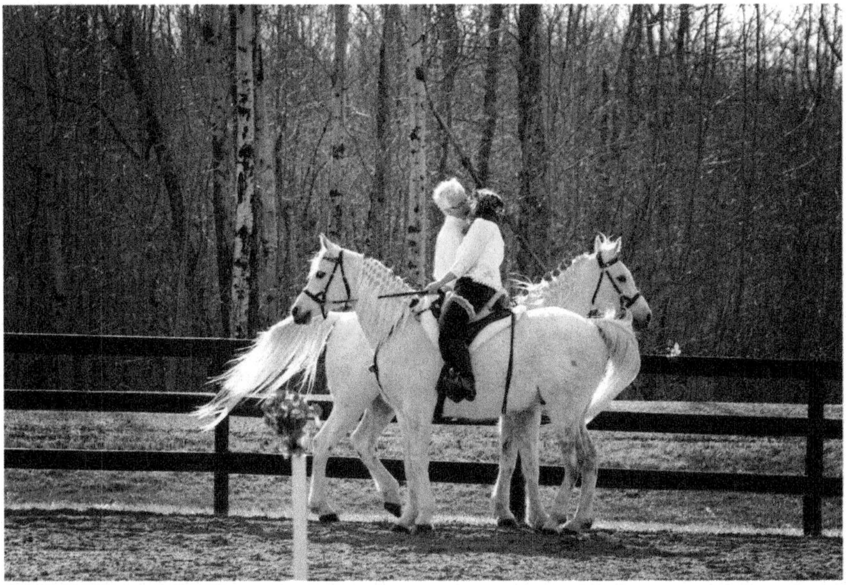

A wedding kiss just before entertaining guests with a musical ride.

This brings us to a discussion of what I believe is a generational difference in the concept of communication. Most people today seem to think that email and text is an efficient and clear communication method. What I have observed, colored by Miguel Ruiz's work in The Fifth Agreement, is that all words are rife with symbolism that reflects each person's past experience and belief systems, and so bare words, on paper or electronic, have completely different meanings and connotations for everyone. The most well-thought-out phrase that I can compose will mean something different to the next person, and will evoke emotions that I cannot foresee no matter how well I think I know that other person. Because of that, meaningful conversation almost never happens unless it is in person. Even in person there is often misunderstanding, because people still interpret through their own lens. Face-to-face can be hard, but it is necessary for the potential of true communication as body language and tone of voice are necessary clues to what is being said and also what is being heard (often not the same).

Yesterday, I did two 90 minute massages, and both clients proved to be the kind of client that I also love to work on. The energy exchange was mutually uplifting and that is the best kind of treatment that can happen, and what I constantly hope to attain. I am opening up more slots now, as I am feeling physically stronger and have actually been gaining weight this week. I still find myself clenching my belly when I am upright, and bringing on my own pain by doing that, so one of my ongoing lessons is to remember to breathe and let it go continuously.

Angie - March 3, 2016 - posted on Facebook

I'm feeling blessed this morning. Yesterday was incredibly emotional with many a breakdown. Sometimes when we let our mind lead instead of our heart we can become focused on "potentials". I've suffered some huge losses in the past few months and I get crippled by fear at times thinking about what more I could lose. Dale is obviously at the top of the list but I could also lose the farm (literally) and my equine friends. That would basically leave me stripped to the core... very scary. So why do I feel blessed? Because there are some amazing people in our lives! Colleen, my late son Cody's love, has helped us in numerous ways and we love her for so many reasons more than her generous spirit. We also are blessed to find that we are having such a profound effect on so many others (as seen in the post below). I hope to remain grateful today.

Angie

Someone had made the realization that they had a lot to be grateful for after reading our posts. We so often found that people were gleaning tidbits out of the posts that applied to much more than this type of situation.

Dale - March 4, 2016

Thursday I spent the whole day struggling to contain my anger, except for the 90 minutes I spent with a client in the afternoon. New solution: work with clients every waking hour, no more anger. Somehow, I don't think that is a practical solution, but thus far nothing has been very practical. We went to see Pete Bernard in the evening, at Healing Connections, and for the second consecutive time, his talk was all about me. I'm sure I was not the only one there that thought so, but it was almost eerie. He talked about getting cancer, and how that motivates me to want change, but yet how I resist changing myself in spite of the fact that getting cancer makes it obvious that something in my life is not working, and NEEDS to change. Someone very close to my heart got cancer and went through treatment which caused them to lose their ability to enjoy food, and I never understood how much that meant until now. I find myself thinking that if I had to face the rest of my life without that enjoyment, why even bother with the healing. Then I remind myself that this is an extremely shallow view of life, but I tell myself to shut up, because the reality is that those little pleasures mean a lot to me. How do I reconcile this? If I figure it out, I might actually be able to move to a place of healing, because as I now realize, the food thing is purely symbolic of all of the things, big and little, that I have not been willing to offer on the altar of change. When we got home, I found I was so emotionally charged from Pete's talk that I was up until 2:00 AM, processing my feelings and thoughts that came up from the evening, and I finally came to the conclusion that yes, I am willing to make change to get change. Yay!

Today would have been my father's 86th birthday, but he passed in 2007 just shy of his 77th birthday. He died of a different cancer than I have, but everything happened even more suddenly for him than it is happening for me, and from first diagnosis to death was a very rapid progression of only weeks. I never got to talk to him about it, as we were not speaking during that time, and by the time I found out he was dying there was no time to go to him even if I had been so inclined, or if he would have invited me. How much we hurt each other over foolish ego on both sides I still have no way of measuring, but I thank Creator for giving me the opportunity to go on a different path that allows me to say the things I need to say, just in case this is the end, and even more importantly, in case it is not.

Today, I feel really good physically, emotionally and spiritually, in spite of not getting enough sleep last night. Taking the time to deal with where I was yesterday and the things that Pete brought up really paid off, and I feel like the progress I am making is validating my whole experience in this journey. Home care social worker came by this morning after my client (another great client experience) and was very helpful around making us aware of some of the programs that we are entitled to receive help from. On the way into the city we stopped at the mailbox and discovered again more help from our friends. We are truly blessed in so many ways, ways that under normal circumstances, we often don't have any awareness of.

Dale - March 5, 2016

Sometimes things happen and we are so focused on the pain we are being "caused" that we cannot see the value that we are being offered. The challenge, just like in this cancer, is to see what benefit could possibly accrue from the situation, let go of the suffering in the situation, and accept the gifts of the situation. Often the gift in a situation that seems valueless is merely the mirror that the Universe holds up so that I can see who I truly am, notice how I am reacting, and choose what really matters. Most of the suffering that I experience from these situations relates to my resistance to what is, or resistance to the reality that I am living in and not accepting, but also not being willing to do the work to change the reality, even though we all have the ability to do that.

Dennis and Mary-Lynn came out this afternoon and took Angie out on a several hour ride on Dude, Mo and Glory, and all three horses behaved admirably. They really are great horses, and of course Dennis and Mary-Lynn are such great friends to gift us their time to exercise our horses, and also to spend a bit of time with us in such a nourishing visit.

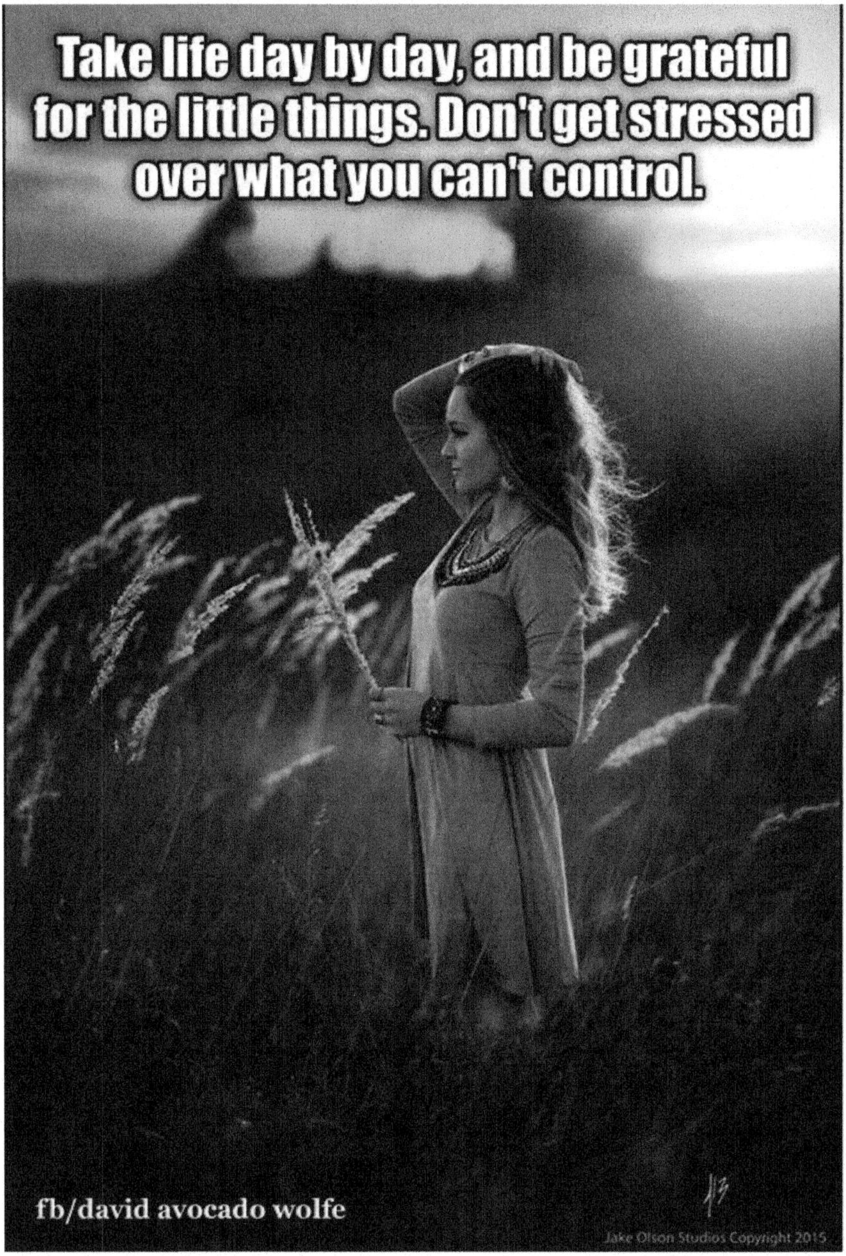
Take life day by day, and be grateful for the little things. Don't get stressed over what you can't control.
fb/david avocado wolfe
Jake Olson Studios Copyright 2015

Today, I am still feeling physically pretty good, but a little tired. I slept ten and a half hours last night, and had a little nap while the others rode, and it seems that just listening to my body and giving it all the nourishment I can and all the time I need to heal is all I really have to do. Of course, I am also paying attention to the emotional and spiritual shifts that are happening for me, and that is an integral part of any healing journey.

Somehow, on Friday when I posted I completely overlooked the incredible energy work that Sabrina offered me at the clinic on Thursday. Thai energy massage is something that I had not experienced to date, and that was also a lovely 90 minute interval where I did not struggle with anger. I believe that the anger I was struggling with related to the process I was going through of releasing many of my feelings around the cancer, and that probably lead to the cancer. Being able to speak about my Dad yesterday, and share insights into how we affected each other was a huge advancement for me, and the result of the shifts I felt after the work with Sabrina and Pete. No matter what happens to me physically in the next while, the emotional and spiritual advancements I have experienced have been totally worth it.

Dale - March 6, 2016

What is the meaning of my life? In other words, what is my purpose for being here at all, what is MY highest purpose? When I agreed to be incarnated, who was I meant to be before I learned to act as I have acted my whole life? These are questions I have asked in the past, with no sense of urgency or even a sense that it was necessary to come up with an answer.

Up until recently, I believed that accumulation of knowledge was the thing that really mattered, and that knowledge would bring wisdom, and wisdom was the most meaningful thing that I could dispense to my clients. Not only have I spent my whole life in a quest for knowledge, but from the time we are babies we are conditioned to respect and seek knowledge. It is the focus, and perhaps even the idol, of our society, but who does it serve? I have come to believe that knowledge is the goal that homogenizes our society, and helps to maintain the status quo.

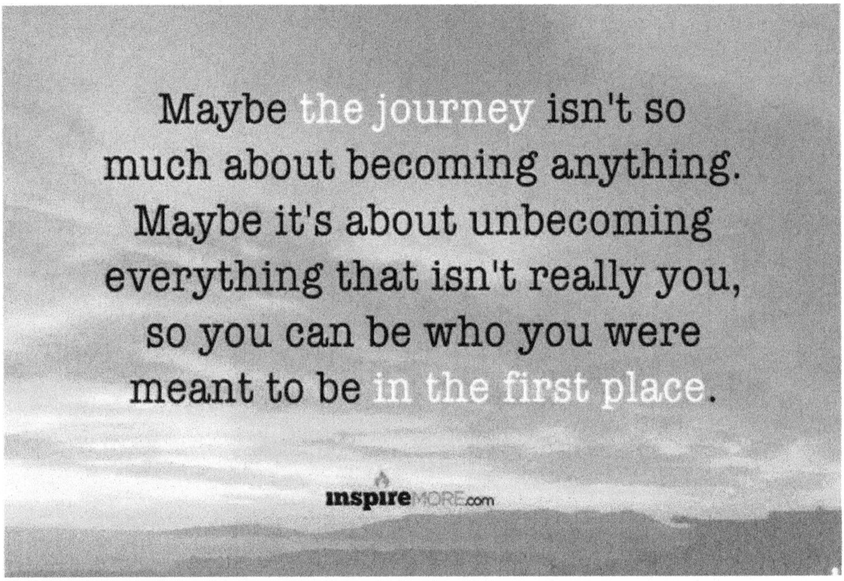
Maybe the journey isn't so much about becoming anything. Maybe it's about unbecoming everything that isn't really you, so you can be who you were meant to be in the first place.
inspireMORE.com

I am starting to see that it is time to shift to a new paradigm, and that perhaps knowledge is not the be-all and end-all that I have always believed it to be. What could be more important than knowledge, you say (as I have said more than once as I have been shifting)? How about TRUTH? And no, in case you are going there, knowledge and Truth are NOT synonymous. Knowledge does not feed the hungry in "underdeveloped" nations or regions. Knowledge does not defeat ISIS. Knowledge does not convince governments or corporations to be responsible to the Earth, or even to people. Truth is the one thing that offers real hope in a world that makes no sense, a world filled with pain and suffering for so many people. Only Truth offers the hope of honest and meaningful change in the direction that this society is going in.

So what's the problem, you say? Knowledge is relatively easy to accumulate. Read a book, take a class, observe nature, experiment, hangout with "wise" people: all these are ways to gather knowledge. Truth, on the other hand, is seldom convenient and almost never comfortable. Truth requires a willingness to change and a willingness to be vulnerable. Truth demands soul-searching, and a peeling away of the veneer of society, and often demands that we go against the crowd, and even against what most of our friends are saying and doing. Truth insists that we examine what we know, prepared to reject everything that does not fit with Truth. It is not an easy journey, this moving towards Truth, but there is nothing else we can move towards that has the potential to change the world we live in.

Dale - March 7, 2016

Angie finally found a comfort food for me that tastes good every time, contains some good nutrition, and has zero negative side effects. She makes an ice cream substitute from frozen fruit, vanilla and coconut milk that is absolutely wonderful, and I believe will be the only ice cream I will ever want for the rest of my life. She really is marvelous (I marvel at her actions, abilities and attitudes).

Today was a good day for nutrition and a bad day for pain. Even with my dose this morning, I spent most of the afternoon at a 6+ on the pain scale, and I think it was because I saw three massage clients this morning/afternoon. I will not be able to do that on a regular basis for the foreseeable future, because that amount of efforting creates tension in what's left of my stomach muscles, and that seems to be the origin of the pain. Nutritionally, by 5:00 I had three juices, a large smoothie, a bowl of chicken soup, and a few home-made nutritional and safe snacks.

Also today we found out at 4:06 PM that the lab at the Tofield hospital closes at 4:00 and there are no exceptions. Argh. The good news is that my BP and temperature are fine, and my GP was only concerned about my current pain level, which we can fix now that I'm home and can relax. Gotta let go of tension, it still seems to want to be my nemesis. I also got the forms signed by my doctor for CPP disability pension, so we will apply for that tomorrow. The rules say that for terminal illnesses they will give us an answer within 48 hours of applying, so we'll see.

Dale P. - Really? My reaction to you is not about you, it is about me.

Nobody can hurt me except me. You do NOT have to be responsible for my feelings.

Kazza H. - I don't interpret this as someone needing to be responsible for another's feelings, but aware or conscientious would be nice. We can't just walk around being dicks (or worse) and never take any ownership of the fact that we are hurting others. What if this was discussing physical violence? I agree that we are responsible for our reactions, but I don't blame another for having feelings that heal better especially when acknowledged.

Dale - Acknowledgement of feelings is great, but in every case we have to take responsibility for our own feelings, no matter what the other person does. Why? Because the ONLY thing we can change is the way that WE respond to others. That does not imply, as you said, that it's ok for me to be oblivious to others, but you are always living in the possibility of interacting with hardhearted and careless people.

YOU ARE THE ONLY PERSON IN YOUR REALITY!

Do you know that you are the only person in your reality? I can see a lot of you wondering what I mean by this statement. In making this statement I am teaching of letting go of everyone and everything else in your reality and living your own life. For many this will be very hard for they have come to rely so much on others. There is a closeness by many to those close to them; and yet, these people are only there for your learning.

WHEN A PERSON TELLS YOU THAT YOU HURT THEM, YOU DON'T GET TO DECIDE THAT YOU DIDN'T.

—LOUIS C.K.

Every soul who comes into your life is a mirror and a teacher. Their purpose is to help you to see the parts of you that need working on. The parts of you that you want to run away from. Many of these people you run away from, yet nobody is an enemy! All who come into your life are there to teach you something or mirror something that you do not want to deal with. Usually these issues have been many incarnations in being.

To you they seem so real, friends, family, enemies, you put names to them, however, they are just teachers and mirrors nothing more and they are the actors in your play that you have created before you came to the Earth plane.

What a shock for many of you to realize this! It is the truth. Only when you realize this and accept it, can you move forward. For when you accept and realize it, you then stop blaming others for your problems and predicaments and accept responsibility for your own life whether good or bad. Nobody is meant to have a bad life, nobody is meant to be unhappy, you make yourself unhappy. You do this by being afraid to live your dreams, by procrastinating about decisions when you should just "Do it'. Spiritual evolvement is about letting go of the fear and doing it. It is about loving yourself despite the fact that you may think others do not.

Remember those whom you think do this are there to mirror for you your lack of confidence and belief in yourself. Once the lesson is learned, the person is no longer in your life, they move away, or you move away. You do not need them anymore, they move out of your play, or you move away from them. All that is negative can be turned into a positive. All you have to do is to decide to change things and be determined and not give in to the Self, whose sole purpose is to try and stop you moving forward.

Spirituality is not about being religious, holy or pious, it is about being true to yourself, only when you do this can you then live life the way it is meant to be. When you see those around you as mirrors and actors on your stage, then the lessons do not seem too hard. They become experiences to learn from, you can actually laugh at them. When you do this, you truly become spiritual. Look upon everyone in your life as a gift, for they truly are, and when they do something that upsets you, ask yourself why you are getting upset. Then, you may be able to see what is needing attention in your life.

~Maitreya

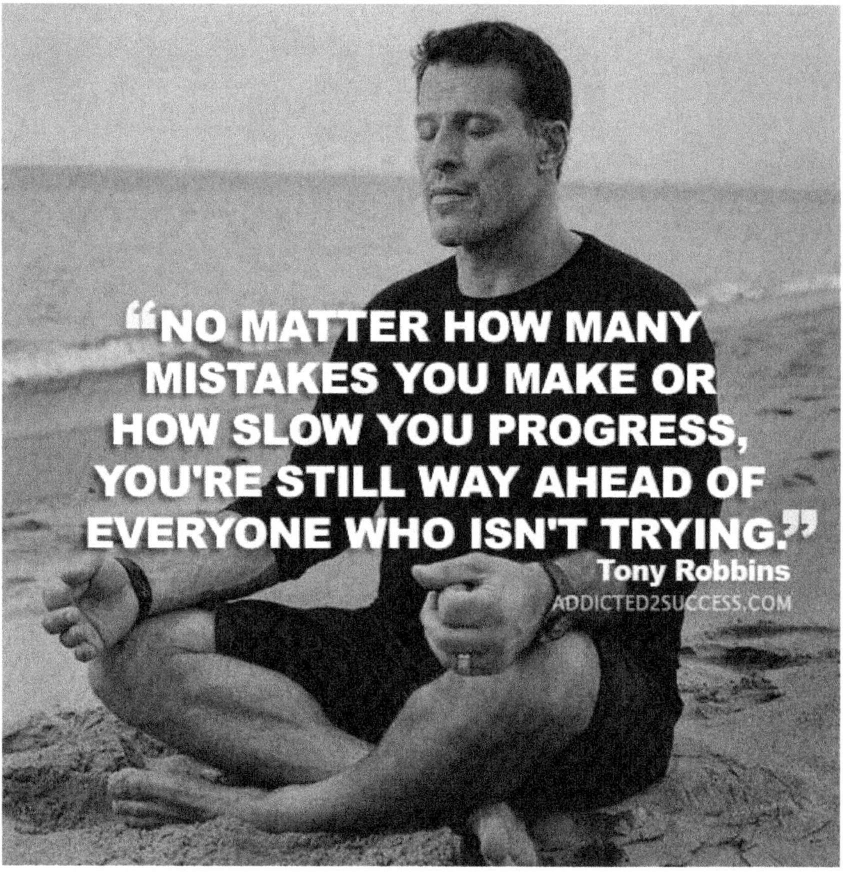
"NO MATTER HOW MANY MISTAKES YOU MAKE OR HOW SLOW YOU PROGRESS, YOU'RE STILL WAY AHEAD OF EVERYONE WHO ISN'T TRYING."
Tony Robbins
ADDICTED2SUCCESS.COM

Dale - March 8 - 10, 2016

The last few days I have simply been struggling with my own journey. It feels like I am close to a breakthrough in relation to the actual cause of this cancer, but also that the closer I get to understanding the root cause, the more my mind resists going there and the angrier I get (at everything and anything). Because of that, I have been quiet on the posting as I spend more time inward than outward. Also, I have tried working a little more this week, to occupy myself, to feed my energy (working has helped raise my energy in the past), and to bring in a little income. That hasn't really worked out so well for me, as I just don't seem to have the energy to put in without repercussions (exhaustion at the end of the day, as well as a tightening of what remains of my stomach muscles, which in turn seems to shut down my ability to take in nutrition).

It's interesting on an intellectual level to observe the constant struggle for balance, so much more evident under these circumstances than it has been in the past. Working with my clients is such a marvelous experience, and so energizing on the emotional and spiritual levels that I want to do it all day long. The balance is that physically, I just could not do it without losing calories that I don't have to spare. This week has been a journey of rediscovering how to work with clients effectively without expending so much physical energy that I am exhausted before the day is done. Part of that has involved actually paying attention to where I am tensing up while still paying attention to my clients. While this has been rewarding, I am glad that I applied for the CPP disability pension this week because I just cannot, at this time anyway, work enough to support us.

Final note for now is that I am receiving energy work from so many of my friends (thank you Cheryl, Chris, Sabrina and Pete), and we are working ever closer to identifying the root cause of the cancer so that I can heal that issue and begin a meaningful recovery in addition to the physical recovery that I am hoping for. Also I am working with my naturopath on a new protocol (in addition to all the things we are already doing) that shows some promise at the physical, emotional and spiritual levels. Thank you Dr. Steinke.

Dale - March 11, 2016

Thursday night: I forgot to mention that on Wednesday, Angie managed to get a little over 2,000 calories in me, and today I felt really good, and when we went to insert the IV, my veins did not try to dodge the needle. Also, today I was over 2,000 calories again. The only downer, and in some aspects it is actually an amazing upper, is that I got a call from Dr. Gutfreund just before we got home tonight (amazing because I was discharged weeks ago, and he is still paying attention to my case). He got the results of my blood test on Tuesday and he is happy that the bilirubin is continuing to fall (110 last week, 70 this week, approaching normal), but he noticed that on Tuesday's test this week my white blood cell count was up, and even in the absence of other symptoms, he wants to make sure that I don't have some kind of infection. We will call Dr. Hackett's office first thing tomorrow and get him to order a blood culture so we will know if I need to be on antibiotics. I've also moved my one appointment tomorrow to Monday morning so I can make myself available for Dr. Hackett.

I also want to clarify something about my anger, which I was talking about in my last post. I am not angry at my body, because my body has not failed me. My body has continued to carry me in the most amazing ways possible, still allowing me to do things that I really should not be able to do at all at this point in time. My body did not betray me in getting this cancer – if anything, I have let my body down by ignoring the issues enough to necessitate this message from the Universe. The cancer, as I have stated before, is merely the message, and the message is that I have a short time to deal with my old issues if I want to achieve what I'm here to do in this lifetime. If I don't, I get to come back and try all over again. So my choice is to thank the cancer, excuse it from the room (the physical changes that I can make), and get to work on my issues so that I can be done with these particular things in THIS lifetime. The anger is partly frustration at my inability to see what it is that I need to see, and I believe it is also part of the process as I work at figuring this all out. I'm even beginning to think that the anger may be a big part of the reason I got the cancer in the first place (I don't actually remember any part of my life where I was not angry inside, with the exception of the time I am working on clients, which I believe comes from me focusing on others and getting out of my head), so getting it out in the open is a major step in releasing it from my life and solving the puzzle.

Finally, today we added N-A-C (N-Acetyl Cysteine), which is a Glutathione precursor, to my protocols. The value of Glutathione is it will help to expel mucus and protect lung tissue. It's an anti-oxidant, and also an immune system booster. This is in response to the expectoration of mucus I've been experiencing this week.

Friday morning: In "Seth Says", this morning, I read of the possibility that my multiple incarnations are happening simultaneously rather than sequentially. That is certainly an interesting possibility, and might explain where emotions and directional changes that seem incongruous with my circumstances may come from. I'm not saying that I'm automatically accepting that as truth, but merely that it is a very interesting hypothesis that gives me some food for meditation (because meditation leads to truth, while thought merely leads to more knowledge) (WOW).

Also this morning Dr. Gutfreund's office called again with some clarification, and faxed us a new requisition for another blood test to see if the WBC is rising. If it is, I will get an antibiotic and otherwise I won't. While I was getting ready this morning CPP office also called to let us know that we had missed one page of the 11 page application for disability pension. Unfortunately it was the page from the doctor and is absolutely necessary, so we faxed it to them so they could complete the preliminary work and we have to pick up the original at the office and get it to them before they will authorize payment. Just as I finished writing this, CPP called back to inform us that they had made a mistake and the original was actually there, so we're good to go. It is retroactive, but there is a 90 day waiting period (weird if I have a 120 day expiry date!) so I'll start getting cheques sometime in April. Yay!

Email from Vera G. Sent to Dale: Friday, March 11, 2016

Hi Dear Dale,

Thank you so very much for seeing the boys yesterday. Such a lovely healing for them. I just wanted to mention something and please forgive me if it may seem shallow. I have read that it could take the body a few months to get to its pre-caffeine state. I know you have much deeper stuff to work out but at least some of the emotions and lack of energy may still be related to that or the missing of the occasional beer. Maybe knowing this you won't be so hard on yourself. I wish you ease. Vera.

Dale - Vera, Thank you so much for both aspects of your message, and no, I don't think it is shallow. Everything affects everything, and the more we are aware of possibilities the more potential we have for progress. There are no details so small as to be unimportant in this journey. Love, Light and Laughter, Dale.

Bernie Sanders was questioned about his spirituality. His reply is as powerful as it is heartfelt: Every great religion in the world — Christianity, Judaism, Islam, Buddhism — essentially comes down to: Do unto others as you would have them do unto you. I believed it when I was a 22-year-old kid getting arrested in Chicago fighting segregation and I've believed it my whole life. That we are in this together — are not just words. The truth is at some level when you hurt, when your children hurt, I hurt. And when my kids hurt, you hurt. And it's very easy to turn our backs on kids who are hungry, or veterans who are sleeping out on the street, and we can develop a psyche, a psychology which is I don't have to worry about them; all I'm going to worry about is myself, I need to make another 5 billion dollars. But I believe that what human nature is about is that everybody in this room impacts everybody else in all kinds of ways that we can't even understand. It's beyond intellect. It's a spiritual, emotional thing. So I believe that when we do the right thing, when we try to treat people with respect and dignity, when we say that child who is hungry is my child ... I think we are more human when we do that, than when we say hey, this whole world , I need more and more, I don't care about anyone else. That's my religion. That's what I believe in. And I think most people around the world, whatever their religion, their color — share that belief. That we are in it together as human beings. And it becomes more and more practical. If we destroy the planet because we don't deal with climate change ... Trust me, we are all in it together, and ... That is my spirituality.'

Dale › Mar 11 not posted on Facebook

Put the bag on when I got up, drained 50 ml of slightly less dark green bile in about one hour, then removed the bag for enema time. Experiencing slight discomfort in the liver area, and mild sharp pangs from the exit point of the stent through my skin, probably from some mild scabbing in the area. More pain for the last three hours, 6.5/10 and better. Drained another 400 ml of dark green/brown bile at 1:30 today. Drained another 500 ml of dark amber bile at 8:00 pm, and another 250 ml of amber fluid at 10:30.

Angie

As Dale was starting to feel less control over his life he started recording more and more information. It began with fluid amounts and later it was detailed accounts of the amounts of pain medications. He also began recording time in military format, which I find is an interesting parallel in regards to control.

Dale - March 12, 2016

Friday: This is shaping up to be an incredibly positive day. Everything that we have touched on today has turned out to be absolutely positive and uplifting. Every phone call was successful, every interaction was polite and uplifting, and all of our scheduling needs were easily met. Not only that, but I look out my kitchen window and the sun is shining and it is another beautiful day. Life is grand, as my brother Jim would say, and I can totally agree with him. Sometimes it is so easy to focus on the problems and the negative implications of events and incidents that we completely ignore the big picture.

OK, so balance – everything has been positive today and the balance is that I have been at a 6.5/10 on the pain scale since 10:00 this morning. I don't know what that is about, or why. I had my meds this morning a little later than usual, but in three hours since I took them the pain has not diminished. I did get my blood test in Tofield, and we will wait to hear from Dr. Gutfreund as to whether I need antibiotics, emergency cholangiogram, or nothing at all. Sometimes the message is just to slow down and stop trying to push so hard, and that may be the bit I am missing here today. It has been a week of regimentation and running here and there, and it has felt like we have little or no time for ourselves all week, so this might be the price. That said, I am looking forward to getting my hair washed and trimmed (thank you Kristie for your kindness and support), getting a treatment from Cheryl (thank you for all you do), and then having a quiet supper with Colleen and Ken (another sincere thank you to two wonderful people).

Saturday: This morning Dr. Gutfreund called and told us that the blood work was good, and in fact he said to Angie that whatever my body was dealing with this week, by Friday it had handled the problem quite impressively. That could be the Goleic or the H2O2 nebulizing, or it could be the N-A-C, or it might even just be my body's ability to heal when I'm aware of what I need to do. Whatever the cause, it means we get Monday off, and don't have to drive anywhere.

Today I am absorbing the energy of my treatment with Cheryl yesterday. In the treatment, my Dad was very present, with some messages for me. I found that I really don't need an apology from him, because I understand that he was doing the best that he could, with the emotional and spiritual tools that he inherited and understood, so that is not a problem. I also understand that he (and Mom) were my choice, and so what I got from them was what I thought, before I came here, would give me the best opportunity to accomplish what I came here for, so I can thank him as well for doing his job to the best of his ability. The one thing I still want from him is to feel that he actually loved me, and that is so far the one thing that I struggle with receiving from him, even now. I will continue to offer him my openness and hope that I can receive that feeling from him still.

Dennis came over and we had a short chat and then he and Angie went out to ride Mo and Dude for a couple of hours, and then apparently to deal with a few minor chores that needed looking after.

Dale - Mar 12 not posted on Facebook

Stomach pain today at a 7/10, so I took some meds, once at 8:30 and again at 11:00. Both times the pain receded almost right away. Took more at 1:30 and the pain receded again, without much of a buzz, which might be just fine for working days. No bag today. Took a prescription pain-killer at 9:00, and then my evening dope.

Dale - March 13, 2016

Starting to feel a little better, finally. The pain is down and I've been able to eat more than the last few days. I must take it easier next week than I did last week, I just cannot push that hard and not suffer. Plus, I get away from meditation time (too tired) and reading/writing time (same reason). Now that I'm approved for disability pension, the money should be a little less of a motivator, and I can continue to see the clients that I choose and can handle.

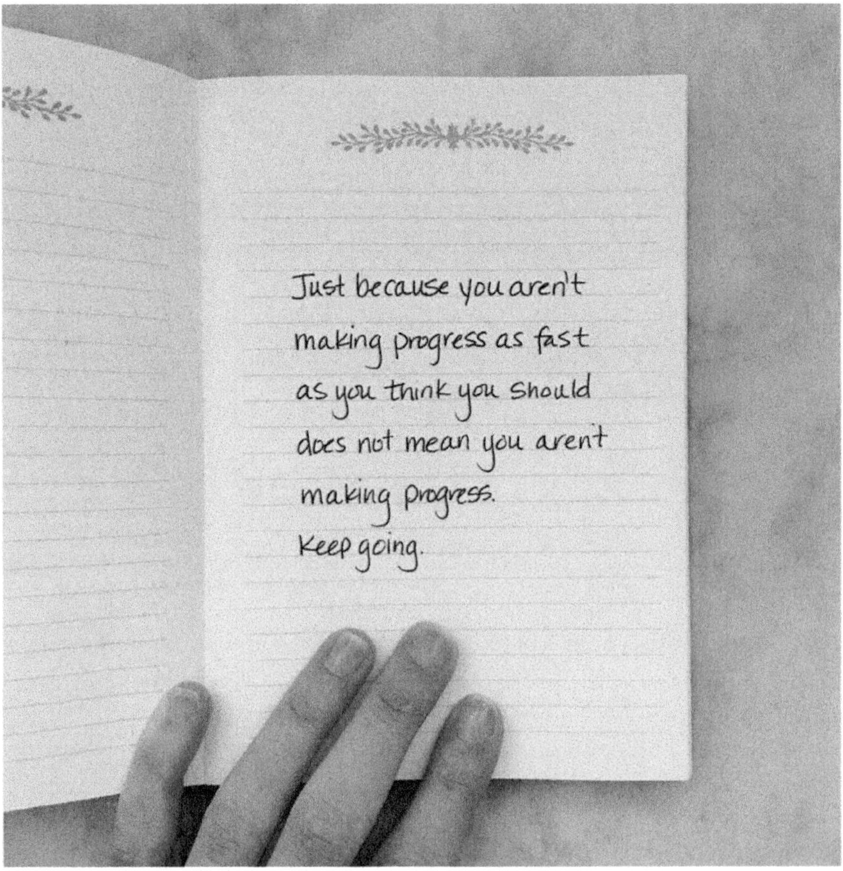
Just because you aren't
making progress as fast
as you think you should
does not mean you aren't
making progress.
Keep going.

Tonight, Angie made me buffalo chicken wings with no chicken included. They were absolutely awesome, and I could see these in my diet even once I can eat more than veggie mush and juice. These were made from cauliflower, almonds, and Frank's hot sauce, and the flavor and texture were remarkable. Had a great smoothie this morning with pineapple and banana, and ate some fruit as well. Maybe a little low on fluids and total nutrition, but an improvement from yesterday.

Spent a bit of time on the phone today reconnecting with friends, then Angie went for a nice 90 minute ride on Dude, while I had my first sauna since the liver stent, and did several meditations. Then I got to sit outside on the south side of the house in the sun for an hour, and that was marvelous too. I feel blessed, and ready for the coming week.

Dale - Mar 13 not posted on Facebook

Drained a total of 750 ml today. Pain all day 6/10.

Dale - March 14, 2016

Tried to manage my time better today. Saw two clients with three hours between them, and did a meditation in the gap. Taking it easy this afternoon, just letting the stomach relax and let go. Will do another meditation shortly, and then try to maintain this pace this week, and see how that goes, I'm hoping I don't have to cut down even more. Also drank more water today, even though there is no nutrition in water, just to try to wash this blockage through so I can start over with the nutrition again on an empty stomach.

Dale - Mar 14 not posted on Facebook

Pain at a lower level today, took the RSO in the evening, drained 150 ml greenish bile.

Dale - March 15 and 16, 2016

Tuesday: Today I feel pretty good, like I'm getting back to normal. Had a good morning, except that I was so dehydrated, even after making a special effort to drink lots yesterday, that I resorbed the entire coffee dose from this morning. That is the first time that has ever happened to me, but there can be no other explanation, especially in light of the fact that my veins were still "mushy" at 10:00 when I arrived for my IV. So, more attention to hydration!

Had my healing session with Shaman Pete today, and the session proved very valuable: I've known about the anger aspect of my condition for some time, but we were able to shed more light on the flip side, that I was apparently oblivious to, which is "unforgiveness". This took me a little by surprise, but I realized almost right away that this might be my sticking point. After some meditation on this, I realized something: There is NOBODY or NOTHING out there that I cannot afford to forgive. So what am I hanging onto? Starting today, I will actively forgive everyone who has ever been a part of my life, or intersected with my life. My life may depend on it.

Wednesday: Continuing today with my "Journey of Forgiveness", which is on one hand simple and on the other hand more complex than I would have thought. I find that there is a complex hierarchy of details to work through on some of my forgiveness projects, but by sticking with each one until I have worked through all of the layers I am finding peace with each of the people I am forgiving. I've even found time and energy to work on forgiving myself for some of my mistakes, and look forward to the day when I can say I no longer harbour any hidden resentments, even towards myself.

Today I saw this poem on Facebook, by Jeff Foster, and I thought it was so appropriate that I just had to repost it with my blog:

IMAGINE...

I do not believe in anything.
I have no religion, and I am not against religion.
I hold no fixed theories about reality, including that one.
I see heaven and hell, karma, reincarnation and the search for enlightenment as beautiful fairy tales.
I have no guru, no lineage, no teacher, and so everything and everyone teaches me.
I see doubt and profound mystery as my most trusted companions.
I walk no path except the one appearing directly in front of me.
I have no home except this sacred moment.

I trust nothing at all, except whatever happens.
I find no meaning in life except the fearless living of it.
I know that today could be my final day.
I feel grateful for all that was given and all that was taken away.
I see the inherent limitation of language and yet love to play with it.
I see the joke in using the words "I", "me" and "mine" and yet delight in using them.
I realise that I am not my story, and realise that even that isn't true.
I find it impossible to say anything about myself, for experience is constantly changing.
I find it effortless to talk about myself, for who I am never changes.
I know that on the deepest level I am profoundly equal to you.
I know that these sentences are pale imitations of truth.

I do not believe in anything.
I have no religion.
Except the in- and out- breaths.
And endlessly deepening wonder.

- Jeff Foster

Dale - March 17, 2016

Cheryl P. - Wow, this is truly beautiful....

Can I ask a question? And, you truly don't have to answer - your and Angie's time is precious right now....

How have you built the life you have; with Angie, with your work, your home and within yourself - if you are harbouring this "level" of resentment? I am blown away by this revelation from you. I believed something else - that you couldn't function at such a level of enlightenment and humanity with such negative feelings behind it. However, on my own journey recently, I have seen how well I have compartmentalized and therefore hidden some of the trash from my past.... Thank you again for posting, I don't say inspiration lightly, it really has meant a lot to hear from you on your journey. My love to you and Angie

Dale - Cheryl, I think that there are several aspects of this that are important. The first is that, as you have discovered, it is quite possible to compartmentalize, especially when the feelings I have are not very attractive. This does not mean I am not aware of the feelings, but it does mean they are not in my face all of the time. The problem with this is that these feelings color many of the things that I experienced, especially outside of my practice (because in my practice I focus so completely on the client that I am outside of my stuff for the most part). The second aspect of this is that having a darker side makes it easier to understand my clients' darker sides. In other words, how can I understand pain if I have never experienced it? I believe that having this "dark secret" has also kept me from feeling superior to anyone else, and that has been both a blessing and a curse. A blessing in that it keeps me humble, and a curse because it has kept me from moving fully into my power as creator of my life. As a final note on this, my relationship with Angie works because we made a conscious choice in the beginning and renewed it throughout our relationship. That choice was to talk about EVERYTHING, to keep no secrets, and to CHOOSE to never take offence from anything the other says or does.

Dale - March 18, 2016

This particular TED talk (Hackschooling makes me happy by Logan LaPlante, TED University of Nevada) was incredibly inspiring to me yesterday, and I thought his 8 piece map of how to "be happy" was particularly succinct. The eight "legs" of happiness are Exercise, Relationships, Diet & Nutrition, Recreation, Time in Nature, Relaxation & Stress Management, Contribution & Service, Religious & Spiritual.

Today was a day off, and I am glad, because I must keep my workload down to less than ten clients a week right now. I am using more Reiki, and also a 'thumper' to take some of the physical load off, and we are seeing a much stronger connection with the clients I am seeing, so I am quite pleased with the direction this is going in. We have an acupuncturist for the clinic, now, and she is also interested in doing a day or two a month out at the ranch, and that is also exciting – to be able to offer those services out here has been a goal of mine for some time. So, in spite of some of the curveballs that life has thrown at us, overall things are moving in a very positive direction.

Dale - March 19, 2016

Tonight we are going to Festival Place to hear Harry Manx perform, just Angie and I on a date night. I'm really looking forward to it, as I've never heard him live but I like what he does on his albums. Also on the agenda today is finishing up the income tax files for 2015 and getting that ready to file, and perhaps getting rid of some excesses out of my workshop – clearing up clutter and simplifying 'stuff'.

I've been thinking a lot about 'unforgiveness', as well as learning to practice the art of forgiveness, and I believe that unforgiveness is rooted deeper in other emotions, emotions like fear (what could happen to me if I don't maintain my barriers) and hate (the motivating force behind the unwillingness to forgive).

Hating an evil, whatever that evil is, is both an excuse and an incentive to create more evil. This is the primary point of breakdown in most religious systems. "Love the sinner but hate the sin" is a saying I have heard many times, and this often degenerates in systemized philosophies to 'hate (or, more commonly, fear) every aspect of the sin, including the sinner'. This is the primary reason that most religious systems are exclusive rather than inclusive. When the message is love, everyone is lifted in their vibration. When the message is hate (or fear), my vibration and the vibration of all around me are lowered, and thought processes degenerate into a cycle of fear and vengeance, whether we are talking religion, politics, or any other point of dissention.

Daisy S. - I think there are not many absolute truths but this is one of them. There is a lovely line in Gates of the Forest by Eli Wiesel, "An act of love may tip the balance". Also absolutely true.

Dale - March 20, 2016

Today I feel pretty good, which is amazing as weekends have tended to be my hardest days for some strange reason. The concert last night was excellent – I have a totally new respect and appreciation for Harry Manx, and I would say if you haven't heard him, and you like a little blues with your folk, you really should check him out. Among other things, he combines an East Indian flavor in instrument and sound that speaks deeply to me.

We had dinner last night at Yoshi, a Japanese restaurant in Sherwood Park, as the Thai place we were going to eat at on Argyll near the casino had closed and converted to a Caribbean restaurant. I really enjoyed the seafood soup, and was able to eat all of the seafood from it, but the noodles were too much and I left them – too much carbohydrates, and probably not very good ones. I am quite pleased with how my taste buds are performing lately – as long as I don't allow my stomach to fill to the point of backing up, I can taste food and it is wonderful. I was also able to have a small glass of white wine before supper, and that also tasted quite good, even if it is not really good for me physically, I felt great for being able to be semi-normal again.

On another encouraging note, I am maintaining my weight. After a steady decline from 180 lbs. down to 130 lbs., from mid-December to the beginning of March, I have levelled out at 130+, and am only varying a little between 133 and 135. This is a welcome stabilization, and tells me that the things WE are doing are paying off. The pain has been worse, in some ways, because even with the meds I am constantly experiencing a level of pain that is aggravating at the least, but it feels like the pain now is related to what is releasing and moving, and that leaves me feeling encouraged by the sense of progress. Also, the ability to eat some normal food is another factor in my generally positive expectations.

Dale - March 21, 2016

Happy first day of spring. And, appropriately, this is the best I've felt on a Monday in quite some time, at least since the second liver stent was installed. Saw a few clients this morning, managing my energy much better than I have been, and then off to see Dr. Hackett who has requested a CT scan to determine what the tumour is doing, and then to my weekly blood test where the tech felt I was looking much better than the last time she saw me. All in all, a good day with many confirmations of the improvements that I am feeling.

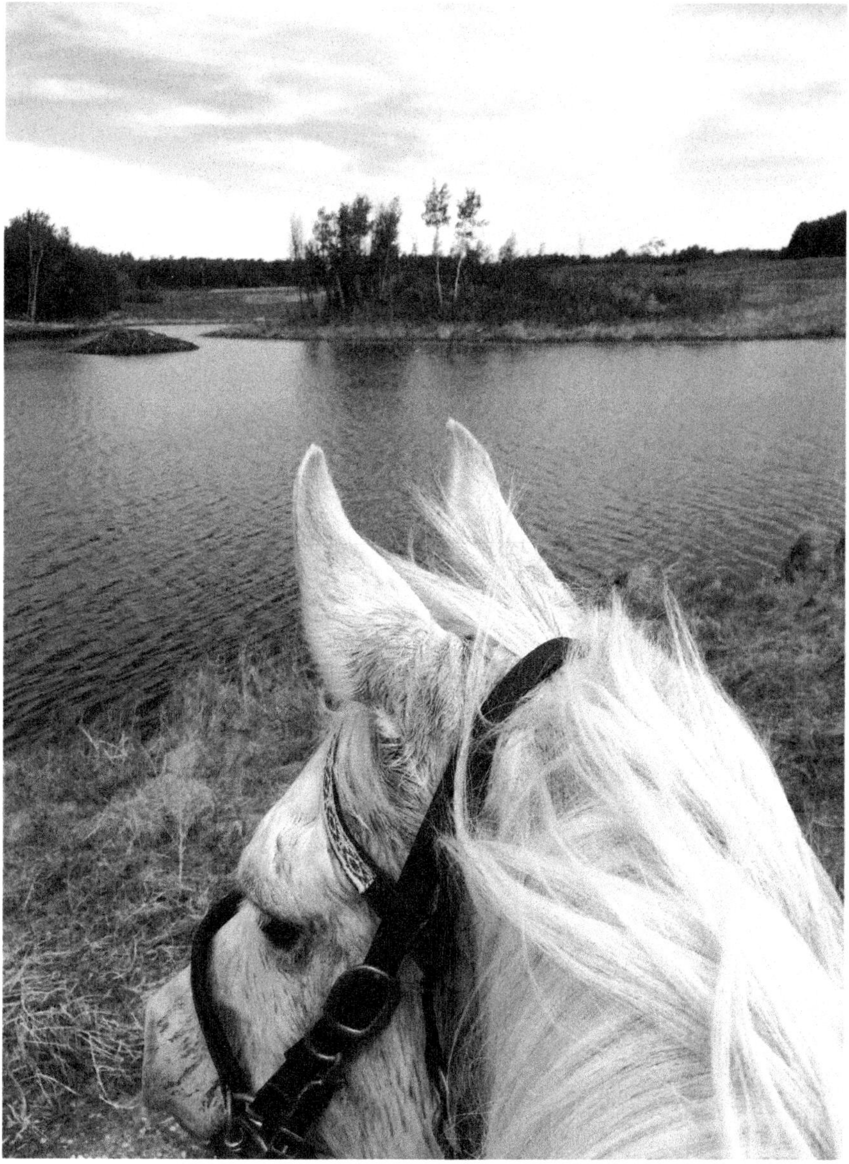

The view from Angie's perspective while out riding Dude.

Today we received a flower arrangement from the Endurance Riders of Alberta club, and it is quite a cheery arrangement. Thank you to the executive and all of the members behind this lovely gift, we appreciate that you are thinking of us in this tough time, and are motivated to want to compete this year. At least Angie will compete for sure, as we are working on all three horses to get them fit, but I don't think I can ride until I get the stent removed, as falling on it could kill me. Hopefully I'll be riding this year, but if not I'll be back with a vengeance in 2017.

Strangely, one of the juices we tried today seems to have made me sick, for the first time in this whole saga, I actually threw up. The good news is that after I eliminated the juice (that we think was the culprit) I stopped feeling sick and totally returned to normal, though I chose to play it safe and all I've had since about 5:00 tonight was a glass of "safe" juice and some home-made "ice cream", neither of which has caused a problem. As I said to Angie the other day, some days this feels like a joy ride strapped naked to the hood of a '72 Impala driven by a drunk that I don't even know. Hopefully back to normal tomorrow.

Angie

At this point in time I had begun riding on a regular basis with my good friend Deb. She was getting Dale's horse Mo, fit for competitions, whether she or Dale would end up riding him. A while back, when Dale and I had a meltdown he suggested I go out with friends just to "get away" for a while. I told him that the thing I needed to "get away" from could not be left behind, this situation resided in my mind and going out would not help. Riding, and being around horses in general, is exactly the thing that COULD help me to escape. Horses require our presence of mind, especially if we want to have them respond to us (and our requests) rather than have the horse making decisions based on their need for survival. They are a herd animal that either leads, or are led by the one who is most aware. Paying attention and being in the moment is what makes us effective when working with horses, and being in the moment is exactly what I needed. I cannot stress the value of being present, enough! In all things! In relationships, in our work and in our lives, this is the moment that matters, not the past or the future. Pain and suffering are greatly reduced when we can stay present, and it determines our past and future experience.

Dale - March 22, 2016

OK, now after the night we had, I am a little amazed at how extreme this roller-coaster ride is. I woke up at 1:40 this morning with so much pressure in my lower abdomen that I thought I just had to urinate, which is normal (three - four times in eight hours of sleep, because of how much liquid I'm drinking). However, the pressure did not alleviate, and when I tried to go back to sleep, the pain ramped up to vary between 9 and 10+/10. I took my one med, which takes about 1 hour to take effect, and then I took one of the very few apo-hydromorphone tablets I filled from Dr. Hackett's prescription. To my extreme surprise, that only took about 15 minutes to take effect, and I had a lovely sleep on the recliner for almost four hours, waking up feeling very stoned for about three hours more. Blessedly, as the drug wore off there was only a very low level of pain, so I have no idea what that was all about. I think that Impala has a turbocharged 454 in it.

Dale - March 23, 2016

SO, a word about apo-hydromorphone. One little tablet (tiny, really) at 1:40 on Tuesday morning and I was still feeling the effects when I went to bed on Tuesday night. While it was great to relieve the pain in the middle of the night, I cannot take a pill that affects me for 24 hours afterward, so I'm going to have to talk to my doctor about something that is effective without staying in my system so long.

Today I need to go for x-rays so they will be able to decide if another endoscope or a new CT scan will be necessary. The problems I had Monday night scared me a little, as that seems like a huge step backwards. Added to the fact that I could not get all my nourishment yesterday or today, I feel like I need to know more definitively what is happening. If these x-rays show nothing needing further study, then I have a CT scan scheduled for April 1 which should tell us what the tumour is doing, and then we will decide whether to order more Goleic or not.

Angie

Dale had previously talked about our having to decide whether or not to order more Goleic (GcMAF) and we had decided to go ahead, in spite of it costing between six and seven thousand dollars for a month's supply. We felt that we had to give it a fair chance rather than quit after just one month. We were in a position to do this only because of the kindness of some close friends. We were so blessed to have friends that loaned us large sums of money and many friends and family who donated to our cause.

Dale - March 24, 2016

Last night I got the call from Dr. Gutfreund, and he sees nothing on the x-rays or blood work that raises any concerns for him. No sign of more or larger tumours and no blockages and no evidence of ruptures anywhere or even major infections. That is good news, and now I will wait for the CT scan April 1 (appropriate?) to find out the status of the tumours, which I believe are stable (or possibly even shrinking). A good sleep tonight and normal nourishment tomorrow is all I am focused on at this moment, so we will see what the night holds.

Here we are on Thursday morning, and the good night's sleep just did not happen – I woke up at 3:20 and that was the end of sleep for me, as my brain kicked in and began to process all of the things that are going on for me. The other possibly unrelated thing is that we watched the Amy Winehouse documentary last night, and I was introduced to a version of Jazz that I had really never heard before, and I liked it. Whether it was her story (sad, moving, and inspiring) or her unique sound I cannot say, but I can say that I might actually be willing to listen to a bit more jazz, especially if we can find someone who sounds anything like her.

I'm still having a hard time putting in enough nutrition, and I have no idea why. The struggle continues. Today was a reasonable day except for the pain level, which was higher all afternoon than I am comfortable with. The meds did not help today, so I just took another apo-hydromorphone, seeing as I have no responsibilities for the next 24 hours +. I'm sitting here waiting for the pain to reduce enough that I can relax, and then hopefully I can eat a little and get a good rest tonight (I almost never have two sleepless nights in a row, thank you).

Dale - March 25, 2016 ("Good Friday")

Good Morning on this Good Friday. I got 6 hours sleep last night, and was awoken by the pain at 5:20 this morning, so I got up and took my meds. It took nearly an hour for the medical marijuana to take the pain down to a manageable level, but I'm doing better now and will start my daily routine. At least Angie was able to sleep for an extra 90 minutes, which I am grateful for. Last night Angie told me that she had been reading something that listed the side-effects of pancreatic cancer, and she was going through the list like 'hair loss, check, bad taste in the mouth, check, bruises easily, check. Oh, wait, these are the side effects of chemotherapy and radiation, which I'm not doing, so why am I demonstrating many of the effects? This might be more than an academic question, but right now it is merely food for thought.

This morning is shaping up well, and I'm feeling better than I have in quite some while. Got the juice down, and then the enemas, and finally the smoothie went down easily as well. Now we're sitting with a friend and I'm having a bowl of Folk Healing soup, which is also going down nicely. I feel pretty blessed today, as she is setting up a Go-Fund-Me account for us, and there is some potential for raising some money to help us be able to continue with this journey with a little less financial pressure.

Had a nice visit with Dell P., then spent some time on the phone with Harry, and then got a call from Cheryl S., who wants to come and work on me tomorrow afternoon. In the meantime, Jean came out and went for a ride with Angie – Angie rode Dude who seems completely recovered from his minor injury last week, and Jean rode Mo, the first time she has ridden him. I got to do a meditation and work on moving the blockage below my stomach, and that feels a lot better now as well. Tonight we will take Jean over to Larry and Doreen's and spend some time with them and Diane, so in all this has definitely been a very Good Friday!

Dale - March 26, 2016

Had a good evening with Larry, Doreen, Jean, Diane and Angie. Ate a little supper, which went down smooth, drank 1 beer (the first one since December 18), had a visit with Larry while the ladies had their Grandmother Moon celebration, and got home about 10:00, feeling good. A good night's sleep tonight and a nice easy day Saturday (and Sunday) and I should be raring to go for next week.

Got to sleep about 11:15 last night, woke up twice to urinate (normal, lately), then woke up at 7:30 with a lot of pain (8/10 at least). Took .5 ml of oil immediately after I got up. Took a hydromorphone by 9:00 because the pain was increasing, and then got the shivers so I bundled up on the bathroom floor (warmest room in the house, set up for my enemas) but I couldn't stop shivering, so Angie bundled me up in a quilt on the floor with my feet on the heat register, and I still couldn't warm up. I was so tense, and the pain just kept ramping up until it was about 15/10, the most pain I've experienced in the last ten years, and I found myself caught between laughter and tears. Finally the pain killers started to kick in, and I moved to the couch bundled up and went to sleep for a couple of hours. Angie said I shook regularly while I was sleeping, and when I awoke, I had a pretty high fever, and some pain in the liver area.

We installed the bile drain bag, Angie made a few calls, and we ended up at Tofield emergency because my temperature wouldn't go down. Blood work, blood cultures (from three separate locations), and x-rays (repeat of Wednesday's images) and I have a biliary infection (bilirubin is up, liver enzymes are up, WBC up) meaning admission to hospital and IV antibiotics every 6 hours. MRSA swabs were done, because I had been more than 24 consecutive hours in a hospital in the last few months, and then consult with Dr. Hackett. He feels that the tumour is actually bigger, but I won't accept that until we see the results of the CT scan on Friday (Apr 1). He did assure me that this has nothing to do with Friday night (Larry, Doreen and Diane please take note) as the infection took a couple of days to develop. Biliary bag accumulated only 200 ml of fluid from noon until about 8:00, but it was the color of used motor oil again, so that's another indicator of some stagnancy there. I also took another hydromorphone at 8, and I'm noticing that they take effect quicker to remove the pain, but I'm getting less of a stone from them, which is good because as much fun as that sounds like, it is not welcome.

Angie

One of the most difficult experiences of this journey was being a witness to the extreme pain that Dale was in and I found myself sobbing uncontrollably. He is a "tough guy", one who can deal with enormous amounts of pain and just slough them off.

I remember an incident about eight years ago where we were putting tension on a fence wire, we had a pry bar inserted into a double wire and were twisting it rather tightly when somehow my grip slipped (if I remember correctly we were alternating handling the pry bar) and the bar spun recklessly out of control whacking Dale squarely in the temple. In the past eight years we've referred to that as the "head-whack-fuck!" incident. The sound was louder than a driver striking a golf ball and there was no question as to how much that hurt but in a matter of moments he was back to work.

Dale - March 27, 2016 (Easter Sunday)

Yesterday, I dozed so much that when it was time to go to sleep I was wide awake, so I read until my Kobo died at a little after midnight. I was awakened at 4:00 for antibiotics IV, then at 6:00 for vitals, then again at 6:40 for PCT check (liver drain), and then finally at 7:00 for shift change and then I was awake for the day. I left the curtains in my room open last night (on purpose) and was able to watch the sunrise, and it is a beautiful day. I took another hydromorphone at 7:30, and am pleased that it is cutting the pain without giving me the heavy stone they originally produced. Breakfast this morning was hot water (for tea), coffee (cannot drink), Jello (cannot eat), apple juice (OK), and a can of ginger ale (trying to avoid pop for lots of reasons). I thank the Universe profusely for Angie, because she is preparing my food for the day while I'm here and will deliver juice, sparkling water and a smoothie when she gets here sometime after 9:00.

Angie and Jean arrived at 10:30, Greg O. stopped by for a minute, Henry and Tina dropped in for ½ hour at 11:00, and Dr. Hackett came by just when they were ready to leave. He's pleased with my progress, but wants me to stay in the hospital at least another day so he can keep me on this particular antibiotic, as my alternative is to come to the hospital four times per 24 hours for the treatment, so we can be sure the infection is eradicated completely. I agree with him, and Angie and I discussed it briefly and decided that I will stay in until he is confident that I'm good to go. That means no clients Monday for sure, and we will have to decide day-by-day what I will do.

Angie and Jean went home to ride, Henry will come by and ride with Angie when he can over the next few months, and Angie has Deb Clary, and Dennis and Mary-Lynn Dickenson to ride with as well. My heart is less broken knowing that my horses are being ridden and that Angie is able to ride regularly. Anyway, after they left, Zach C. dropped in for a visit, and then Cheryl and Danny S. dropped in for a short visit. I'm really feeling the love from all these friends, but now I have a few hours of quiet to be able to bring my blog up to date and just relax. Angie will be back around 6:00 to spend a couple of hours with me, and hopefully I will sleep well tonight.

Dale - March 28 and 29, 2016

Monday was a day of trying to stabilize. Sunday I was feeling pretty good, but maybe that was only relative to what Saturday had been like, with the extreme pain caused by the infection around the liver and the bile leakage. Also, I had lots of encouragement Sunday, with all of the company and their good wishes. Anyway, I again was overoptimistic on Sunday, and tried to eat too much too soon, which left me unable to eat properly on Monday, and again brought me to an awareness of what a fine balance it is to try to manage caloric intake with mass and density of food. I don't know how Angie manages to maintain her equilibrium as she tries to balance encouraging me without appearing to nag me about what I put in, but without her I would be lost.

We got on to a regular schedule with the IV antibiotics and the pain meds, finally, and so I am not sinking into pain, taking a pill, and then struggling to come out of the pain. I get a hydromorphone with each IV now, and so I never fall into the area of 7+ on the pain scale and I am able to stay mentally present when I am awake now. This week Angie cancelled all of my appointments, so I can spend the week healing and getting back to some semblance of normal, and that is what I should have done. I just really do not know how to be if I am not working – in some ways, the work I do is my identity, but I also think I am still struggling with the whole concept of self-worth. If I cannot do the work, what is the value of me being here? Toughest level of self-examination I have dug into yet, and I guess this is the week for it.

I told Angie that if the CT on Friday shows that the tumour is growing, I'm going to enter the endurance ride on April 15 in Okotoks, because that might be the last opportunity I have to compete. She said that she didn't think that was a good idea, as I don't have the strength to ride for five or six hours, or to sit the trot for any length of time, and I said I don't have to trot, I just have to stay on until the finish, as long as I finish before the time deadline I will feel like I've won. I don't have to come first, I'd be happy with just finishing, even if I'm dead last. We both realized at the same time what I had said, and had a real good laugh about that, continuing to joke about having to tie me into the saddle and then on to the idea that the horse has to be in a certain condition to complete the event, but there is no rule that says that the rider has to be alive at the end. Even gallows humor is better than no humor, and I think that Lauren, our homecare nurse, who had dropped in to check up on me just a few moments before that, appreciated the jokes.

As I write this, it is 7:00 on Tuesday, and I had the best sleep I've had in several days, and am feeling like I could leave the hospital today. Recovering at home, without having to run all over the place with appointments, etc. will be good for me, although I have to say that of all my hospital stays in the last several months, this has been the most restful I have experienced. If any of you ever need to be admitted, I highly recommend Tofield hospital – it is truly quiet and restful, and the staff here is so very supportive (as I have experienced with every hospital interaction I have had since this whole thing started).

I got sent home today at 1:00, after lunch and my IV and hydromorphone, and we got home to a message from Beaver County emergency services telling us that all fire permits have been suspended as there is a fire ban on now. I believe that is one of the earliest fire bans that I can remember. Angie got to ride this afternoon on Dude while Deb rode out on Mo, and Angie told me that the ground is drying up nicely and things should be great by this weekend. Tomorrow I'll try to spend a little more time outside after we come back from Tofield and my IV antibiotic, which I have to go in for daily.

Dale included this in his document, I'm unsure of its origin:

I am not a Christian. I am the Christ Consciousness. One is religion, which separates, one is Unity. Jesus was not Christian, he held the Christ consciousness, so do the other Ascended Masters. The crucifixion is only symbolic, to release your lower self. The Resurrection is a symbol to be born again into the Christ Consciousness where there is no death. With no belief in death, what could we possibly fear? Without fear, there is only Love.

Private message –

Hi Dale! I was just reading your post for 28/29th and I thought I would text you, letting you know where your value has helped me currently and in the past. Your guidance has allowed me to feel a certain physical or spiritual presence in people. For example, when I'm working on the sacrum and how that could translate into their lives, being open and using certain language to open people up in a way. Before I would feel a "flag" or cue from a person's body and maybe look past it but now I realize almost everything is connected in this work, and in life with people.

Following little subtleties turn into big moves, or big work with clients and, with the people you love. Rather than looking past these things, one might inquire, "How has this changed for you?", or "What does that feel like for you right now". Anyways, my purpose is to connect with people, and you've given me a big tool that I will always hold in my belt to assist with connecting, getting me closer to people in their journey. It's nice to think that, in many ways, how we affect our friends and loved ones will always live on through them when we are all gone from this place.

Not to say I anticipate you leaving here anytime soon, but I thought you might feel pride in the fact that you've touched/changed my life, and I'm sure many others, given the 8ish years I've known you. Oh also, when I tell people how I honestly feel about a shitty meal, or speaking my truth I think of you and Angie. Lol. Thank you for just being there and being yourselves over the last while I've known ya. - Kim M.

Angie

Dale mentioned "gallows humour", we sure did have a great many laughs during this whole episode. I'm not sure when it started but somewhere along the line we began saying "what's the worst thing that could happen?" It applied to anything that seemed as though we were somehow at risk. It made light of an almost unbearable situation. It really helps to laugh about the things you want to cry about, and either way, it helps to release those pent up emotions. Releasing emotions periodically prevents those eruptions that rival Mt. Vesuvius.

Dale - March 30 – April 03, 2016

Wednesday: Today I want to talk again about all of the people in our lives. A friend of ours suggested a GoFundMe campaign when she realized our financial situation, and after thinking about it for a while, we decided that could be a good idea, so we 'approved' it and helped her to go ahead and set it up. Immediately afterwards, I went back into the hospital for 4 days, and I didn't forget the idea, but I did forget to follow up on it, so I checked up on it this morning now that I am home, and I have to say that I am almost overwhelmed at the generosity of people that know us. I truly did not expect the response that we have received, and I have to say that this is really going to help, as it takes the pressure off of me feeling like I have to work even though I don't always feel capable of expending the energy. In summary, again I want to say thank you from the bottom of my heart to all who have contributed financially as well as those who have supported us in so many other ways. You have made this bearable when it might not have been.

Angie and I have been talking about the idea that if you knew you were going to die in a year, what would you spend your time doing. We both recognize that we all waste a lot of time doing things that are not productive, so what other choices can we make? It is really easy to think that I would spend all kinds of time and energy on really uplifting things, or really spiritual things, or even on 'humanitarian' things (all of which would be uplifting). The truth of the matter is that I spend most of my time physically, mentally and spiritually exhausted, and so I "waste" time doing mindless or easy things that don't have much value in the long run. I feel ashamed to have to admit this, but I think it is the reality for many people who are going through the process of dealing with severe illness or disability.

Friday: Today is my birthday, and I wasn't truly sure I would see this day. I woke up to a smile and a happy birthday from the woman I love, who looks after me in ways that I never in my life previous to this imagined being looked after. Typically since Wednesday, I spent a couple of hours in the morning getting myself going with Angie's help, then went to the Tofield hospital for my IV antibiotic (that takes a couple of hours to get done). Angie filled my prescription for hydro-morphone, as I am at this time dependant on them for pain management. I have noticed that the medical marijuana leaves me feeling a bit more irritable than I like, so I use it as backup when needed instead of as my go to solution. After the hospital, we spent a bit of time relaxing at home and then headed into the city for a celebration. We picked up a birthday cake at Hazeldean Bakery, pickup up Jean and dropped the cake off at Rosie's, and then went to Syphay on Calgary Trail for dinner with 11 of our closest friends. Two hours later (8:30) we went over to Rosie's for three hours of karaoke with our friends from dinner and another ten good friends. Angie and I each sang four or five songs, and everyone had a good time. Partway through the evening, Angie served up the birthday cake, which was amazing. Home around midnight and right to bed. It was a great day.

Angie

Dale did not mention that this was the day he went for a CT scan to determine what was happening with the tumour. I knew in my heart what the news would be but did not voice my opinion to Dale. We were often encouraged by small improvements on a day to day basis however, he was in more pain and he was less able to eat which both seemed like clues.

He did mention that he was experiencing hair loss though, and it was driving him crazy because he was always covered in hair. So, on the spur of the moment he decided to get a haircut. I tried to reach our wonderful Kristie but I was unsuccessful, so it was off to the barbershop. I cannot begin to describe the feeling in the pit of my stomach as we entered the establishment; much too fancy a word for this seedy, smelly, gathering place for old men. Dale was 63 but he was no "old man" and the idea of him getting a brush cut literally made me feel sick. I had in fact seen him with hair that short, he had once shaved it all off several years before. This was much different! It already felt like he was vanishing before my eyes. Not like a magic act at all, it was a slow but seemingly steady process. A pound every few days, less energy and less ability to do the things he had been so skilled at. But this was to be a sudden change that seemed huge and unthinkable in my eyes. I could not watch as it was happening, in fact I did not look at him for about 30 minutes after we left the barbershop. Finally he said "why can't you look at me, what's wrong?" It came out of me like a flood, I had to pull the car over to the side of the road. While I had not fully realized what was really so "wrong" I put it all together once I started trying to explain it. I bawled, Dale held me close and I was able to release some tension that I'd been carrying and put it all into perspective. After that I looked at him and he was still my handsome man, in spite of the big change and all was good.

Dale used to remind me of the Vitruvian Man made famous by Leonardo Da Vinci. He was symmetrical and proportionate. He was handsome and healthy, carrying just the right amount of weight. I believe he would have lived to be 90 or 100 quite easily if not for this one glitch. As time went on and Dale lost more and more weight I started noticing small things almost daily. It started with us saying he'd become a great "lesson in anatomy". You could see ligaments and tendons and muscle definition that body builders never attain. Then the ribs became flat looking. And who would think that you could lose flesh from the ear lobes and the nose? I began to see a stranger when I saw previous photos of Dale, I was getting used to the new image. It took quite a while afterwards but eventually I began to remember the previous healthy version rather than "Skeleton Dale".

As cancer takes its toll on the body it changes a lot of other things about the person who is suffering with it. They become much more dependent, maybe a bit cranky and in Dale's case obsessive about little things that would not have mattered at all before. I wouldn't say it changed his personality but it most certainly changed MY experience of him. I had to often remind myself that in spite of everything he was still the Dale that I loved, at least in spirit. I think his experience of me must have been different as well. I believe that I was more like a mother/nurse to him near the end.

Dale - Saturday: Tina sent me a link to this little bit by Satyen Raja. Angie and I first met Satyen in early 2008, as he was heading up the Warrior-Sage group. We went to a weekend intensive at the Nakiska Lodge near Banff, and then that winter we went to another intensive in Los Angeles, and we decided that while the idea was good, the organization wasn't really for us. That being said, Satyen put out some very good things, and I liked the potential of this article:

Article from Satyen Raja (edited by Dale Pierce): Straight for the Jugular

Death is where you start on the path of the Warrior-Sage. Not the morbid death of recoil or rotting bodies, but the full embrace of Death that slaps awake any drifting from true purpose. It's obvious we all will face it, or is it? You will be alive until you die, so you will never know death anyways while alive until your last breathe, whatever comes next is whatever it is, if it is at all. Like a fast forwarding full immersion video, the discipline is to feel the complete death of all your dreams, hopes, ambitions, health, wealth, victories, defeats and freedoms. You feel the complete death of all your loved ones, that's the hardest for many. You feel the total death of yourself even from existence itself. Some of you are fortunate to have faced or be facing real imminent death. Perhaps through illness or sudden accident Death is all too real (and surreal as well). It's definite and indefinite due to the inevitable and unknown it evokes. Our primal fear is the finality of self which is, never the less, the most avoided confrontation for most, the paradoxical effect is having a dead life. The old joke of dying in your 20s and being buried in your 90s is funny for a while.

Where you may last wish to go and hide is the first stone to uncover and turn to. So face Death feeling it fully coming at you from every angle, even within your cells. Let all the fears have their hey-day and feel it all while staying wide open through your loss and tears. Expand, breath, body and presence when death is felt near, never let it contract you. When death is closest for real, feel what you must do to live and die completely without regrets, and do it without fail. With courage do what you need to do to give and receive love without holding back, without excuses. Let Death unshackle you from delay and procrastination. Let Death be your impeccability and follow-through coach. Let Death be your "be in the moment" guru. Let Death`s ever too closeness, be your awareness pin prick to look for, appreciate and foster a Life filled with Life, a Life filled with living beyond death`s despotism over your deepest soul`s calling. Ultimately Death may reveal the secret to Life itself.

Sunday: Just to give you an idea of what our life has been like this week, let me tell you what our day looked like today. We woke and got up at 6:15 this morning, and spent the next 45 minutes getting my morning juice and vitamins and minerals into me. Then it was off to the bathroom for more than 90 minutes for enemas, etc., then shave and other grooming. Then we changed my bandages around the stoma for the PCT, which took another ½ hour, and was fairly painful even though Angie is as careful as is possible. Dress and gather up what we need and off to the hospital at about 11:20 for IV. Today was antibiotics and saline because I was a bit under-hydrated, and I got to have a nice long nap while all that was going in, so we didn't get back home until just after 3:00. Angie finally gets a bit of time for herself to ride with Deb on our two boys, and so I had a bit of quiet time until she came in just after 6:00. Angie gets to go right back to work finishing laundry and then making supper, and we will probably relax for a few hours this evening before heading to bed shortly after 9:00.

Tomorrow, I need to get blood work at the hospital in Tofield, then IV antibiotics again (every day until at least Tuesday), then a meeting with Dr. Hackett to find out the results of the scan on Friday and the blood work on Monday. Then we have the rest of the day to make some decisions about the future, depending on all of these results. No predictions at this time.

Finally, I just want to apologize for not posting for a few days. Since I've been on the regular hydro-morphone dose, I've found it harder to write than it used to be, but hopefully we are past that stage and can get back to regular blog posts.

Dale - April 04, 2016

Today was extremely weird for me. I woke up at 1:30 with a little pain, took my meds, urinated and then went to sleep sitting up on the couch so my stomach would drain better. At 5:30, I awoke again in discomfort and realized that something was happening that I had not experienced this calendar year – I had to have a bowel movement without having had an enema. And it was an incredible movement, especially considering that I had an enema every day for the past month. I thought that was a turning point for me, but 15 minutes later I had to run to the bathroom again and I spewed my supper from last night, which actually felt almost as good as the bowel movement. Took pain meds again, and then went back to bed and slept another three hours, until 9:15. Skipped the enemas this morning (didn't seem to be much point) and did some reading, Doreen dropped in for a brief visit, and we headed to Tofield about 12:15.

As we were coming into Tofield, there had been a serious accident at the highway exit for town. Fire trucks, ambulances and police had the road blocked off, and at least two ambulances went into Tofield to the health centre, which meant almost surely my procedures would be delayed somewhat. Got my blood work done right away, but ended up waiting almost an hour for the IV because of the backlog (outpatients and emergency are the same department). Fortunately, my doctor was the on-call physician, so if I was late for my 2:30 appointment, so was he. Anyway, saw the doctor at 3:30, and he confirmed what we had suspected, which was that the tumour was not shrinking. What we didn't suspect was that it had actually grown by 50% since the last scan. He also upped my pain meds, and cancelled the antibiotic IV, as he felt that had done its job. So now we have tomorrow off, and will begin to try to create a plan of action based on this new information, decide what protocols to continue with, and what to do about the clinic as well as other needs for the future.

Just realized that I neglected to mention a couple of little details from Friday April 1. I was getting so frustrated with the amount of hair I was losing, pretty much a handful a day, that I went to a barber in Camrose and got what turned out to be a brush cut. It was a little more extreme than I had intended, but it got the job done. And finally, when we were back home after lunch, Cheryl came out and gifted me another Reiki treatment. I do have wonderful friends.

Angie

I had a way of separating the time periods before and after we found out that the tumour was still growing. The first period we were "trying" and the last period we were "dying". It was as simple as that. For those first 3 months I couldn't have tried any harder, I did everything in my power to save the man I loved so much. And then, when we got the word, my mission in life was to keep him as comfortable as possible.

I had also realized and I'm not sure exactly when I remembered that Dale had said something to me one day last summer when all was still well (at least as far as we knew). Out of the blue he said "I feel like I'm done here". I said "Huh? What do you mean?" He went on to explain that it was just a weird feeling he had, nothing more, nothing wrong, not depressed or unhappy, he just felt as though his time here was done. We discussed it for a while and when we were satisfied that we'd dissected it, we put the thought back on the shelf and left it there until I pulled it back down for further examination. When I re-evaluated it, I realized that he must've known on some deeper level and if that was so,

I had to accept it as truth. I also recalled how I'd felt during our first trip to the emergency ward, and realized that I had also known. And that led to acceptance. Not that any part of me wanted it that way, it just is what it is... period.

It's interesting, as I re-read these posts, to notice little things that I missed when they were happening. Dale said the tumour had not shrunk "as WE suspected" but I don't remember ever sharing my thoughts with him. Even his posts had not indicated that he didn't believe that the tumour was shrinking. Perhaps we had pondered that and I had given myself away and perhaps this story was so much "ours" that he used the word "we" in most cases without even thinking. It's sort of like when people say "we're having a baby" when most assuredly only one person in a couple actual "has" the baby. In the end, and in both cases, it really does involve both parties.

Dale - April 05, 2016

Tuesday I'm happy to report that the new pain meds are appearing to be quite successful. Instead of two mg of hydro-morphone every four hours, Dr. Hackett has prescribed a slightly different form with six mg every 12 hours, and I had the first one at 9:30 last night and that let me sleep through the night pain free. The only thing I did wrong in that was that I forgot to turn down the heat on my bed warmer, so I woke up at 2:00 this morning quite hot and sweaty. Once I took care of that I slept through until 6:00 with no pain, so I know what to do tonight. I still have the two mg pills for emergency purposes, but twice a day is so much more convenient that if they continue to control the pain I will be quite happy with this system. I also have the medical marijuana prescription as another backup for instant relief.

Angie and I are both experiencing a sense of relief over having a final diagnosis, and we are both oddly OK with that diagnosis. Part of the reason, I believe, is that we now know that the only thing that can change this is what we do directly ourselves, and that nothing coming from outside of us can change any of the things that could still happen. So now, I live or die based solely on my actions, my inner work, and what the universe (the Divine) has in store for me. That also means that even if I do the inner work, this may be my time to pass from this world, and that is quite fine if it is what happens. While I am not actively seeking to die, I am ready to if that is what comes next, as I KNOW beyond any doubt that my physical death is not the end of my existence. My main regret is that I may not get to ride in another competition this lifetime, but I intend to go and crew for Angie at least once or twice this summer.

Sent to Dale in a private message by a cousin -

Hi Dale! April 5 today. One of your posts talked of a doctor giving you the date of April 15 as an 'expiry date' for your flesh. Has anything changed regarding that? My heart is with you on this journey you are taking. You seem to have lots of love & support in your wellness community. What a blessing! You have tapped into a circle of people that love and accept you as you are. Rare! Good for you! I know that you know, and I can't go one more day without reaching out to you to affirm something you do already know. Which is, that along with your friends, your Creator, Father God, loves you too. Loves and accepts you as you are. You were so smart to leave religion behind. I have too! Religion does not represent the heart of our Father God very well at all - nor the greatness of His love for us. I wonder if perhaps you have felt God whispering His Love to your heart in the quiet times? He's not shouting at you - that's not the way He woos us unto Himself. He's more gentle, patient, quiet. But you feel His Presence, right? You feel Him hovering over your bed. You sense Him when it's quiet; when you can quiet the distractions. He's waiting, listening, smiling, waiting some more. He's gently calling your name. He has declared that you are His and He is yours. He declared that at your birth. When your mother was holding you in her arms, God smiled broadly and declared 'that's My boy!' You have always been His. And He has always wanted to be a good, good Father to you, for you. As I pray for you I weep as I feel Father God's heart aching for you to let Him love you. Ya, aching. That's all He wants. No tricks. No treats. No 'works'. He loves you. And He wants you to receive His love and love Him back. That's it. And as you know, the only way to the Father is through His Son, Jesus Christ. And that your soul knows very well. One step, two words. One step of faith towards the heart of the Father. Two words, "I believe". I feel like even the angels are holding their breath waiting to exhale, waiting for your decision. And it is your decision and yours alone. No one is twisting your arm. Only the Presence of God hovering over you. Loving you. Smiling at you. Waiting for you. Accepting you. And respecting your decision. You believe Father God loves you or you don't. Simple. Very simple. One step. Two words. All eternity is holding its breath waiting...for that one step, two words. And if you choose to do that, all heaven will EXPLODE in thunderous joy and laughter! And when we do all get to Heaven, truly it will be a day of rejoicing! Wouldn't be the same without you dear cousin. I trust you receive this greeting in the spirit of love and unity with which it is sent. Peace be yours. Love, cousin

Dale on Mo, doing what he loved to do.

Dale - I read your message this morning, and wanted to reply to it but I must have hit the wrong button because it disappeared. However, from memory, I will attempt to address your comments. It appears to me that you have not abandoned religion in favor of spirituality, because you still seem to be convinced that the bible is the word of god, and you seem to espouse many of the beliefs of the church we grew up in, in spite of the evidence that the bible, and the church's viewpoint on salvation, are all manufactured by early church leaders as methods to control the masses, and also books of the bible were selected based on the political needs of the 4th and 5th century Roman empire (see council of Nicea, for one). Where are all the texts written by the female followers of Jesus? Where are the texts that didn't agree with the church of the time and its political agenda? Why did god supposedly have nothing worth recording to say after the new testament? While I appreciate your enthusiasm in speaking your beliefs, I personally believe that you are naive in your understanding of religion vs. spirituality, and I am not interested in your corrupted (by the very church that created this false paradigm) viewpoint of god, and Jesus' role in the bringing of spiritual messages to a very needy earth. If you spent more time in communication with god in the listening mode, you might find yourself closer to the truth.

Cousin - Dale! Good to hear from you! I am happy to see that although you used a lower case 'g' for God you used an upper case 'J' for Jesus. Yay Jesus! You still respect Him. Warms my heart. And actually just this morning - as I was praying for you - God's message to me was that I should quiet my heart in His presence (the listening mode of which you speak) and immerse myself in His Word. Because even though it does suck that the women who so faithfully followed Jesus are hardly even mentioned in the Bible, Jesus did elevate them to a place of prominence back in Bible times and The Word still is alive and active and like an arrow never misses its target. Which in your case is your heart. God still loves you even if you don't love Him back. Isn't that just kooky? I would still prefer for you to spend eternity in Heaven with me and your Mom. What do you believe will happen to your spirit man when you die? Does your doctor still predict that is only days away from happening to you? What do you predict would happen if you shouted out the Name JESUS as in The Christ, the only begotten Son of God who has his Finger on your pulse right now?

Angie

*Perhaps Dale's response could be considered as somewhat harsh but please remember that this was not the only person who felt the need to "save" him. He received many other communications that shared a similar message. By this time, and as he was losing more and more control of his life, he was beginning to lose patience with these "well meaning" people. As he mentioned in an earlier post, where he referenced the teachings of Don Miguel, "*we defeat ourselves when we deny someone simple respect*". Dale most certainly felt disrespected each time he received these attempts at "conversion". He had studied and even considered a path in religion, and he was firm in his current beliefs.*

He and I were on the same page in regards to the matter. Even though my parents never attended church (both were disillusioned by past experiences) I was enrolled in a "separate school" because they still considered themselves as Catholic. Even as a teenager I questioned the world, and wanted more information than I was provided by the nuns who taught religion. I was regularly sent out of class because they were unable to answer my queries. It seemed to me that they were uncomfortable about not having any answers.

For the sake of clarity, I appreciate any person who has a strong belief system and I respect that. I only ask that you respect mine.

Dale - April 06, 2016

Posted by another cousin of Dale's –

Terrence P. - I, too, am not afraid of the end of this chapter. But that doesn't stop me from having some trepidation about the unknown on the other side. My faith is strong, but being a man of reason, there is unfortunately no data upon which to base a strong sense of confidence. I must admit that I DO have a sense of fear. Not immobilizing, but there nonetheless. Walking this stretch of the Red Road with you (although separated by miles) seems to have a cathartic effect for me - a surprising serendipity!

Dale - I hear you, cuz, and I would say that there is nothing wrong with feeling what you feel. Having been dead once already (1975), and close enough a couple of more times, and having had several out of body experiences (most notably while isolation tanking), I can honestly say that my sampling of the other side has left me with a high level of confidence and no fear. I recognize that this puts me in the minority. We came into the city today to clean up some things around the business. We did some shopping and banking, and at 2:00 PM we are meeting with our landlord, naturopath and friend Dr. Wayne Steinke to discuss what we will do with the business. One of the issues we have is that if we keep the business open, we will have to pay something over $1,700.00 this month alone in licensing and insurance, and none of that would be refundable if we closed later, so we have to carefully consider our options, especially with me bringing in no income at this time. I will continue this post after our meeting today.

Angie

It's unfortunate that Dale felt he had to bring in all the income but since we sold the lunch truck the revenue from massage and our business was the only source of income we had. All of the funds from the sale of the truck went into Enerchi Massage and Wellness Centre. My "job" was to support through managing, cleaning, providing reception, marketing, etc. It was a very necessary role but one that does not generate any income directly. Once Dale was ill my job was caring for him, a very important job but not a real money maker. Again I'd like to express my gratitude to all of the wonderful people who helped us out.

Dale - April 07, 2016

Well, we had our meeting with Wayne yesterday afternoon, and as he has been throughout our relationship, he was extremely supportive. He fully seems to understand our position, and has offered us any support that we need as we transition out of the business. We will try to close the office and get all of our stuff out of there before the end of the month, as well as leave anything that he could use so that at least we can pay him back partially for his support of us. Now the task is going to be to try to shut everything down in an orderly fashion and dissolve the limited company. I also want to contact all of my clients and let them know that I am available at home on a non-professional basis for the remainder of my time in this life. One of the interesting aspects that Wayne pointed out is that perhaps with all of the pressure of the business removed, we may see a reduction of stress that could have a positive effect on my progress, and I agree with him there. He also reminded me of the work of Dr. Hammer on the emotional basis for cancers, and encouraged me to look more deeply into the aspects of pancreatic cancer that may revolve around an "indigestible morsel" (emotionally or spiritually) that I already have some thoughts about. As a final thought on the business, Angie and I both want to say that we are both quite proud of the success that we created, and pleased with the realization of our dream of creating a wellness centre where we could work together towards a common goal, in the short time we had before this health challenge made it impossible to continue, and neither of us sees this as our failure to create and operate the business or the dream.

Last night I had an interesting experience. At about 9:30 Angie and I were discussing whether or not I could take my six mg dose, as I was feeling quite needy from a pain perspective. All day I had been plagued with a nagging fear that things were much worse than they had been, because I just was not able to be pain-free at all, and as we were debating whether I could take my daily meds then or should wait until 10:00, we had the sudden realization that I had completely missed my morning dose, partly because of the timing of our leaving for the city, and the need to space the Lax-a-day two hours from other meds. I had the most incredible combination of relief and frustration that I have experienced in a while. Relief at the realization that the pain I had felt all day was not because things were worse, but merely a result of the missed medication, and frustration that we were so busy that I never realized that I had skipped the meds, and also at the realization that I could survive a day, however uncomfortably, without them. Crazy.

On another note, I want to say that again I am uplifted and supported by the incredible messages of support and love that we continue to receive from our friends. Harry, Lori, Cynthia, Larry, Dennis, Mary-Lynn, Lynne, Leah, Tina, Henry, Debbie, Gale, Suzanne, Tammie, and so many others (forgive me if I've not mentioned you by name) in the past couple of days, have sent us simple but extraordinarily meaningful thoughts of love and support that leave me feeling like this world still has a chance at hope when there are people like you remaining in it.

Dale - April 08, 2016

Zach C. - I've had a rough year. My life fell apart and I hit rock bottom, health wise, work wise and personal life with friends. I have been fighting my way back to be a better person. I am completely different than I was 8 months ago. Though it still weighs heavy on my heart, I will not let me hold me back. My path to healing myself and picking up the pieces has not been easy but I've pulled through. Thanks to my team. Though it saddens me they some people won't talk anymore or try to fix things. I owe a huge thanks to my mentor and friend Dale who has helped me tremendously on my path to my dream since day one. I owe a special thanks to a certain woman who has made me realize my dream is right in front of me by living her dream. I also owe a thanks to Kenzie for helping bringing my training/coaching skills forward. I've sacrificed a lot to get where I am. Including time with my family, although I am distant and never able to spend time with them I still love and care about them. A lot of what I do is not for myself, it is mostly for them. I feel their love and support.

Dale - April 8 and 9, 2016

The last couple of days we have been very busy cataloguing the clinic materials for the sale, and getting the house prepared for me to be able to stay here instead of in the hospital (if it comes to that). Also, as I've been learning to relax at home (that's a skill I had never mastered, and still may not! LOL!), I've spent a lot of time listening to the music that Angie and I have collected over the years. I had forgotten how much I used to enjoy just listening to random music my whole life long!

One of the things we have at home is an Ultramatic bed that Angie's dad bought and left here, but we have not been able to get the control to work, and there are no "buttons" on the bed itself. We were able to contact the company, and for a couple of hundred dollars we are going to receive a replacement control and junction box that should make the bed fully functional again (much like a hospital bed). Hopefully I can still figure out how to install the "upgrade".

I am amazed at how many texts, CDs and DVDs I have related to the practice of massage and acupressure. For those of you interested, they will all be available at our sale April 22 & 23, as well as the massage supplies and items of décor. Please plan on coming down for the sale if there is anything that interests you at all.

Again, the support of my loving friends and clients has been borderline unbelievable. Since we announced the closure, the response has been more than we can easily keep up with, so if you don't get a timely reply, or any reply, please rest assured that this is not because I don't appreciate you, but more a function of my lagging energy levels. I love every one of my friends and clients, and I am more grateful for you than I am for anything that I "own". I will try to keep up with replies, but there are always some that seem to get missed, but know that my heart sings every time I hear from one of you.

Angie

Music is the key to my soul. I find that music can open up raw emotions and allow them to surface, and escape, usually through my tear ducts. Just one of the songs that touch me deeply is "I'm So Glad I Met You" by Royal Wood.

Dale - April 10 - 17, 2016

Someone else's experience that Dale shared –

Glenn C. - Hi everyone. I have not updated my Cancer fight. The last time I was getting a lot of high 5s for winning the battle. And like all things in the cancer war chest it can change in a heartbeat. Early March I fell severely ill. The tube that drains the liver became blocked and my bilirubin went from normal 21 to 100. They put in a small stint and it didn't hold. 2 days later they put in a larger plastic stint. My count was up to137 and the pain was through the roof. My goal through all of this is to get back to Mexico. We came to hospital on Saturday night. With pain again after a hundred tests they changed the stint to a steel one but still in pain. Last night they found my calcium is through the roof. All the doctors are trying to make sure I get to Mexico. Amazing, a bunch of fluids and it should relieve pain. I have been on antibiotics and pain killers for 2 weeks. Everyone's prayers and thoughts are needed as we start this fight again with more tumours in lower abdominal area. So may the words of the Lord speak to this crazy cancer.

Dale - I hear you, Glenn, I am experiencing similar liver issues with my pancreatic cancer. I find myself less and less interested in the physical issues and more and more involved in dealing with the spiritual and emotional aspects of my life. Physically, I have never seen anything as unpredictable (from my perspective, although not, apparently, from the medical perspective) as this journey has been.

Monday (11): Mom, Linda and Wilf came out and spent the day yesterday, and I was having the best weekend day that I have had in a long time, and having my third good day in a row both pain and food-wise. I also weighed myself this morning after the enemas and have gained another pound and am back up to 129 lbs. I'm eating lots today, and able to enjoy the time with my family, so that is very satisfying. Also, we've had some interesting phone calls from some people who are interested in the clinic as a future for themselves, and that may help us out as well as helping them. Monday morning, and I feel GREAT! Best weekend since I got the diagnosis.

Now I'm writing on Sunday, April 17. I have not posted for a whole week, and I apologize to my faithful "followers" (no religious barb intended), but I have not stopped posting because I've been depressed or in too much pain, or any other reason that I can pinpoint easily. It has been a busy week and a hectic week, but all in all the most up and down I've had since Angie, Cody and I went to San Francisco last November and rode the rollercoasters. After a GREAT weekend, I continued to feel pretty good into the week, which was a pleasant surprise, but I have been relatively confused all week as well, which I attribute to the hydromorphone, as I am using almost no medical marijuana at all. This is interesting, because of course I've always believed that regular pot use "dumbed" you down and prescription drugs are better for your brain.

Anyway, Monday Kylah came out to the ranch for a visit with Melissa, and we updated them on the direction things were going. They both seemed pleased to hear that the clinic would not be shutting down after all, and that of course has been the ongoing theme all week with all of our guests and friends. Zach also came out Monday and was able to do some physical work for me that I have just not had the energy for. A little bit of yard cleanup can make a disproportionately large improvement in the way I feel, as I look out and see things being spruced up, especially as spring can be so messy in the yard. Went into Tofield ALL BY MYSELF and got my blood work done, picked up a parcel at the post office, met Dennis for coffee, and got home. Of course the pleasant weather has been quite a bonus for me this spring (though I am worried about the crops and fires this year), and my mood has been helped by just being able to enjoy the outdoors without freezing my butt off.

Tuesday we met with Tiiu McLim, and both Angie and I liked her right off the bat. We discussed where we were with the clinic, what we had as far as plans, and the potential for her participation. I found myself trusting her right away, which was a pleasant realization, and I felt that we and she were all moving quickly towards being much more open than we had planned. In the end, she was going to discuss the plans with her husband Tuesday evening, and they would come by Wednesday evening so he could meet us and see the place after he got home from work. This was great because Cuihong had a client at 4:00 on Wednesday, after which Angie and I could go and have a bit of supper and maybe have our long-delayed sit-down with my friend Day, and then get back to the clinic and meet with Tiiu and her husband. So very cool to just have all of these things fall into place, like this was the Universe telling us that we were moving in the right direction. We got a pleasant surprise just before we left the clinic as Tiara (Tiiu's friend) and her husband dropped in to see the place briefly, and we found ourselves liking them as well! In the end, Tiiu decided to work things out with us and her husband was on board without needing to meet us at this point. How wonder-filled I am when we find the flow, and I'm so glad we're all learning to go with it instead of constantly needing to direct it.

Wednesday went as planned and we did have supper at Syphay on Jasper with Day. It was so absolutely incredibly wonderful to spend a couple of hours with Angie and Day together, to see them connect so simply, and to know that the two women outside of my family that have had the most positive effect on my life could be friends. I could write lots about how they have done this, but that is for another time, and I just want to leave it at this: I believe that these two women were in my life exactly when I needed them, and I can only hope that my effect on them has been half as uplifting and moving as their effect on me.

Thursday I went to Camrose all by myself again. You may think it is strange for me to put it this way, but the issue is that I have to manage the timing of my meds so that I am not driving impaired while also ensuring that I am not in too much pain, and that has been the challenge. So far, I am pleased to have been able to do this, because that frees Angie up to ride with Deb or Henry, or Dennis, or even by herself, and it helps me to know that she is free to do that without having to constantly look after all of the details of my time management. So anyway, I went to Camrose and had a lovely acupuncture/acupressure treatment with Colleen, and then back home.

Friday, I was still feeling pretty good, but I was in a bit of pain right from when I got up in the morning. The farrier came, and Angie was tied up with him from 9:00 until almost noon. Lauren came to bring supplies and check up on me, and I was in more pain than I really wanted to deal with, even with the med combination I had taken, and I had not been able to put anything more than juice in all morning, so she recommended I get to the doctor, meaning emergency in Tofield as Dr. Hackett was not available. However, Harry and Lori were on their way up from Calgary for a brief visit and I couldn't get hold of them, Angie was tied up with the farrier, and so I decided to wait a bit. After Lauren left, I ended up throwing up all of the juices I had taken all morning, and then I felt quite a bit better. Angie came in, Harry and Lori arrived, and I was OK for a short visit with minimal pain, but after they left it was into Tofield for me. At emergency, they were prepared for me (thank you, Lauren), and Dr. Muneer had left orders for pain relief and hydration (thank you Dr. Muneer) and the staff looked after me quite quickly, installing a subcutaneous port in my right shoulder for injection of the liquid form of hydromorphone, a port for IV in my left arm (more difficult with my dehydrated veins), and started IV saline to rehydrate me as well as the hydromorphone injection for pain relief. I now understand the attraction of drug users to some of the hard drugs, as what I have read about their reaction seems to be what I experienced with this. Instant relief, followed by a period of euphoria, is not something I have ever experienced before, and I was quite grateful to have that at this time.

Saturday was another really good day for me, but it started out awkwardly at best. I pulled the subcutaneous site out of my arm accidentally at 6:00 AM, and had to call the homecare nurse to get it replaced so she could give me my injection for Saturday AM, but once we had that looked after, the day went well. I ended up spending the afternoon outside on the lawn swing on the south side of the house, in the sun, and for the first time in a long time I was not cold. Later in the afternoon we lit a fire in the fireplace between the apple trees, and we were able to sit out there for quite a while together and enjoy the sun, the air, the fire, the horses and each other for quite a bit longer. I sat in shorts and sun-tanned for a while, and then covered up before I got burnt (not my usual first day in the sun for a summer), and all in all it was quite pleasant. This week I have spent more time listening to music and reading than I can remember doing for a long time, and it was good. Between the visits and phone calls from friends, the progress with the sale of the clinic, time with Angie and Chester(our dog), and general relaxation I would say that this has been one of the most nourishing weeks I have experienced lately.

Dale enjoying lunch on the trail in 2012 with Chester by his side.

The bottom line at this point is that I have come to a point of surrender to the concept of death in a much more real way than the abstract acceptance I have had. While not actively pursuing the act, and while absolutely being open to the possibility of a miracle, I realize at that visceral level that my time here is now quite limited without that miracle. Strangely, I am still OK with the idea, and I hope that my passing will not be too painful for the ones that I will leave behind, but the next little while will be a time of farewells. This should be seen by all as a blessing, and I have decided that in answer to the age old question, yes, I would prefer to know the time of my death (at least approximately) rather than be taken by surprise. So please, don't try to comfort me, I don't need that very much. I am confident that I know where I am going, and I am comfortable with that. Feel free to say what you need to say to me, and to joke about life and death, and just be who you are around me as this progresses. We never know: as unpredictable as life is, I may still end up being here for a long time to come. In the meantime, I am going to enjoy life to the maximum I can, and spend it with the people I love while I can. Hopefully, I'll see you all in the next little while.

Cousin P. - Dale, your last post asked people to say what they needed to you because you have accepted that you are facing death. First of all I'd like to say that I am so glad that we were able to reconnect, however briefly. I regret that we were out of touch for so many years. I have followed your posts in awe that you were able to articulate so honestly what you went through to come to this place of peace and acceptance. I want to ask you about something that is purely selfish but I think it will bother me for a long time if I don't clarify this. When we spoke on the phone, you said that the person I am now sounded like a much better person than the old Patti. Perhaps you just meant that I used to be religious and I'm not any more. But if you meant that I had been unkind or hurt you in some way, I would like to know. If you have time to answer this, Dale, I'll be grateful, but if you don't, I'll understand. Much love to you and Angie.

Dale - Short answer is that in no way have you ever caused me pain or suffering, except that I wished I had been in a position to warn you about my perception of B. (not that you would have probably listened). I always liked you, but regret not getting to know you better much, much sooner in our lives. More later if you are OK with this, if not don't hesitate to clarify for me. Love to you from Angie and I.

Cousin P. - Hah! I wish I'd been able to listen to your perception of B. I think, because I'd lived in six different homes after my parents died, I was searching for some stability and I thought marrying B. would give it to me. That turned out well, didn't it? I'm really happy to hear I did not cause you any pain. As far as "more later", I would love to hear more from you, on any topic including your thoughts on my life, your life, life in general. It seems to me that you have gained wisdom from living your life, whereas I'm still filled with a lot of anger. The anger might be appropriate but I have trouble letting go and moving on, even though I know the anger hurts me more than it hurts the person it's directed at. When people are mean to me (that sounds so childish), it bothers me for years. I want to let go but I don't seem to be able to. To make matters worse, every year I add new people I'm mad at. I'm not sure but I think you might be able to help me with this. Again, please don't let my request be a burden to you. Answer only if you feel up to it.

Dale - Two books I have read that have given me an immense amount of insight into exactly the questions you have raised here. "The Untethered Soul" by Michael Singer, and "The Fifth Agreement" by Don Miguel Ruiz are both gold mines. The number one lesson I have learned, from so many life experiences and messages I have heard, is that I don't need to be perfect to have a positive effect on the world. Live the change that you would like to see in your world.

Kathy N. - Hi Dale, yup, I'm one of your followers and I always look for your posts. Riding 25 miles with you two years ago left a wonderful impression on me. I felt your positivity and kind spirit so quickly. You are one of those rare people that is easy to connect with in a very short amount of time. I still hope for a miracle for you, but perhaps there have been some miracles along this journey already. Angie sounds like a miracle in your life, as you are in hers, it sounds. I remember the first time I met you two. We were at the Tees ride and you had your "just married" sign in your camper. We chuckled about it because as we saw you and Angie in your lawn chairs, your vibe was one of knowing each other forever. I'm guessing that you have. Thank you for sharing all that you have in your posts. You have inspired me, have shown such strength. I am glad Emily and I met you, that you came over and sang with us on Emily's 16th birthday. I still plan to see you somewhere in this life, and the next life. Love and hugs to you and Angie.

Angie

At this point Dale had outlasted his potential "expiry date", although you could say that he was, "best before" this date.

Dale - April 18, 2016

A brief news flash for any of my relatives that are related through the Abe Martens arm of the family (or interested for any reason). In the process of going through all of my books over the last weeks, I came across a King James Thompsom's Reference Bible (1929 edition) that I used in Northwest Bible College in the early 1970s and since, that originally belonged to Grampa Martens from some much earlier date. If anyone is interested in having this bible (family heirloom, historical document, excellent reference bible, or any other reason) please contact me as soon as you can, because I would like to see this rehomed rather than discarded.

Judy C. (Ohm Therapeutics class with Samantha) That's so great you were able to sell it. I have been sending u prayers and good energy. You are a wonderful amazing person and your loving and kind spirit touched me deeply at the course. You have been in my heart and my prayers every day. No matter what happens you are love ....and you are loved ...and really at the end of the day that's all that truly matters for all of us. Take good care my friend.

Dale - April 19 -23, 2016

In these last few days, I have received so many messages around the importance of LOVE as the unifying factor in my universe. As well as public messages which have come through Facebook and emails, etc. I have also received a seemingly out of proportion amount of private messages along those same lines. Someone close to me recently told me that they were trying to figure out what they could say to me, and they came to the realization that the only thing that mattered, and the only thing that was needed, was to express their love. Nothing else creates meaningful comfort, and nothing else will survive this transition, and I thank you all for bringing this so clearly into the story that we are now writing as I prepare to withdraw from this world. In the end, what is the last thing I want to say to you? I love you. That is all there is, and that is all that is needed. Even though the end is not here yet, I want to leave this thought with all of you. Whether our relationship has seemed loving or stormy, positive or negative, uplifting or depressing, you have all been part of my transition from unenlightened to approaching enlightenment, and I have learned to love you all for your contributions to my life.

Physically, this week has been another week of adaptation and struggle, as I come to terms with the pain control medications and how that affects my systemic motility. Everything from digestion to bladder release seems to hinge on the amount of pain control I receive, and the struggle is to maintain enough nourishment to prevent starvation while I try to live with as little pain as is reasonable. The frustration is still focussed on how much all of this affects what I can eat, as my appetite is still calling for food that is tasty and nourishing (not always the same foods). So in all of this, my weight is now fluctuating in the 120 lbs. – 129 lbs. range, which is quite ridiculous to me.

The other thing that I am noticing is that all of my ability to figure things out and be in control of my world intellectually seems to be depressed by the meds I am taking. I never thought that this would ever become an issue for me, and it is really hard for me to accept this loss of mental acuity that I have always been quite proud of (dirty little secret?). I thank all that is meaningful (again and again) that I have Angie and a few other friends to keep me on track when I start to slide a bit on this slippery road.

As we finalize the remaining items to be sold in the clinic garage sale, I am reminded of all the people that have been instrumental in taking me from a person interested in massage in 2004 to the competent (I accept this label) massage therapist that I was in 2015. People who inspired me and people who taught me, fellow students and clients, teachers whose courses I never took but were instrumental in shaping my thoughts on energy work. The list would go on and on, and I won't try to write them all down, but you should know that if you are part of the body work world in any way, you probably had some influence on me, and therefore also on others out there. Keep up the work – the world needs you all in ways that have never before been so important.

I wanted to include notes that I made while reading "Seth Speaks", because the book had lots to say that opened my mind to some of the aspects of universal energy that I hadn't really considered before. For example, Seth says that illness and suffering are the result of misdirection of creative energy, and that the only real purpose of suffering is to teach you how to stop suffering. I like that, but it takes a bit of contemplation to come to terms with that idea when we are so programmed to think that suffering is a result of our misdeeds. If we can make that effort though, I believe the reward will be much greater than we would expect, because in learning this technique we can apply it to other aspects of our lives and it will 'snowball'.

Dell P. - You are so right in your observation that the only thing that matters in life and remains after a loved one's passing is love. I speak from an all too vast experience. I've also learned that depression can bring its own kind of gift (try not to fight it Dale). As you experience this uncomfortable feeling it leads to a very deep understanding. I'm not speaking of clinical depression. That's something totally different. Yours maybe drug induced but some I'm sure is an honest feeling of loss. Loss of all that could have been. Dreams unfulfilled. It is legit and part of the whole. A life well lived should be whole. It remains a mystery why this is so necessary but looking at all the great lives lived it becomes apparent that this is so. You have brought so much comfort and care to so very many Dale. You have lived and dreamed well. Although we are the masters of our own ship to some degree we don't have the final say. I hope you give yourself permission to feel this loss without recrimination. Just know that your bravery to open and bare your soul has left a huge impact on many people and I'm sure will have far reaching impart on many others. You are loved Dale on so many different levels. Travel with a light heart knowing this. Just received this Dale, from my sister in law living in Nanaimo BC: Dell, I have just read Dale's essay and am very moved by it. In the following statement, he has given me a gift -- "Whether our relationship has seemed loving or stormy, positive or negative, uplifting or depressing, you have all been part of my transition from unenlightened to approaching enlightenment, and I have learned to love you all for your contributions to my life." Will I learn to love "all" regardless of the relationship? Will I recognize their contribution? Dale is already enlightened. Though I do not know him, I feel like I do and thank him.

Heather G. - I know it's been said many times but Thank You for including us in this journey. Trying to find the right words is so tough but I can't imagine not telling you what you mean to me. I'm not sure how long we've known each other, maybe 10 years? I credit myself with basically discovering you (hahaha narcissistic - I know but this is my story). Ask anyone I know- I have sung your praises to and referred practically everyone I know to you. When I'm crooked and hurting there's no other practitioner out there who can 'fix' me. I know ours is a professional relationship but you became so very important to me. You may not realize it but you have been instrumental in my happiness. One time I was on your table, everything out of whack and sore and you told me I had to deal with whatever it was that I was carrying around for far too long. Of course, you didn't put it that way, you are much more sensitive than that. I just want you to know that you played a big part in me making the changes I really needed to. I may be a tough nut to crack but I did hear you that day. Loud and clear.

Thank you! Much love Heather

Judy S. - I am sending much love and light to both you and Angie! It is so wonderful that you found each other and are able to journey together. We may count ourselves very fortunate to find such a friend and mate in life! Although our paths crossed only briefly, I feel I have learned much about strength and courage from you as you have shared your journey with us. Thank you for being you and for all that you have done! You have made a difference to all of us!

Daisy S. - You are so right, Dale and you put it so beautifully: in the end there is only how much you loved that counts. Sometimes we walk into a room & unexpectedly come face to face with someone who holds a bit of our soul & does so for always. There are miracles everywhere; know that whatever happens you are one.

Carol L. - I love you Dale. We became friends back in the day because we have a soul connection that I value dearly. It had been many years since we last saw each other, and when we re-connected a couple of years ago it was like no time had passed at all. We were able to pick up where we left off. It was fun to see that we had both evolved in to the same direction in life (you working as a massage therapist/energy healer & me as an energy healer). I have many fond memories of our times together when we were young. You have made a positive difference in this world Dale & should be proud of your accomplishments. Your print will remain here forever. Happy trails Dale in your new life! Love you forever!

Samantha J. - You always share such wisdom that I know comes from the depth of your Soul. May we all experience and embrace such Grace when we come to the end of our days. You probably never considered that you would become "this kind of teacher" for so many, Dale … but there it is. You are loved. You are Love.

Email from husband and wife clients –

Hold on steady and strong, Here's the dawn coming on won't be long, Then the sun will come shining through, To show me the place I once knew.
Fare thee well, Fare thee well and adieu, Fare thee well, With this song I'll be gone, Fare thee well. (chorus)
The old man's here and he's fine, He has come here from years down the line, He has

come to bring peace to all times for the few, He has come to bring life to the new. Fare thee well ...
Hold on steady and strong, Here's the dawn coming on won't be long, Oh its easy to stand in the light with pain, In the light I will ever remain. Fare thee well ... (Ian Tyson, Dale we love you too. Fare thee well. G. & M. A.)

Angie - April 20, 2016 - posted on Facebook

This one came up on my playlist this morning. It totally opened up the floodgates. Ever since he was small Cody always identified with Superman, he felt immortal. And he lives on in spirit and in our hearts. Then came Dale, my other Superman. He is my hero. And, it's not easy to be me.

"SUPERMAN" - FIVE FOR FIGHTING - "SUPERMAN (It's Not Easy)"

Patti B. - I can believe it's not easy being you right now, Angie. I hope there are people around you to love and support you. Thank you for the amazing care you have given my dear cousin. I hope to meet you someday.

Angie

Thank you Patti. I do have an amazing support group of my own. Not all of them are nearby but they are always close.

Dell P. - Angie, how fortunate you are to have experience two Supermen in your life. It seems both have revealed your hidden identity of Wonder Woman. For that you truly are. It brings to mind the old adage "to whom much is given much is required". I almost hate that saying but find it to be true. You are an amazingly giving lady and Super in your own right.

Angie

Thank you Dell. Having heard your story I know that you too qualify for the Super hero status.

Dale - April 24, 2016

It's now Sunday morning, and I'm sitting here hallucinating about a floor drain in Joyce's kitchen in San Jose, Costa Rica in February, 1993. What The ?? I can imagine no connection between now and then, and yet here it is. If you can help me out with this, please do as I am totally baffled by it.

Dale - April 25-26, 2016.

The comments I received on my last post (from April 19-23) opened me up like nothing I have received before. Today has been a most amazing day -

Our darling Kim and Jake had a baby girl yesterday (April 24). We have been waiting for her arrival and even though she is a couple of days early, we are both excited and grateful for her safe delivery. 5:00 AM is the witching hour. Feelings of mortality, of how ethereal my connection to life on this plane is, and how easy it would be to disconnect, seem much easier to sit with at this time of the day. Last night was a time of just bathing in the presence of the love that Angie and I share, and the realization that that time in this life is very near to its end. Not a time of sadness, but more a time of preparing to close a chapter. That visceral realization that one phase is ending and another will soon be opening. Actually, and now especially with the arrival of McKinley Erica W., this is feeling more and more like the beginning of something fresh and new, a new season of joy and life, and new potential.

Linda N. - Hi Dale... good news about Kim and Jake's baby... good for them! Thanks for letting us all know. I must tell you, it is really special that you share your thoughts with us. You are a very wise man and an inspiration to all. I remember when Angie first met you... I knew you were soul mates from the very start. You two have shared a life that anyone would envy. Even though I have only met you a few times, I feel like I have known you all my life and I am so thankful for that connection. I can see from the posts from your many friends and family, that you are loved by all and have touched many lives. I am sorry that you have had to suffer so much these past months... there is no answer as to why that has to be. Despite your struggles with pain, you still radiate love, kindness, hope and so many other qualities... you are truly an amazing man! Oh... and did I mention you have a GREAT sense of humour? lol (just as sick as mine!). Hang in there buddy... much love and peace to you... thinking of you and Angie EVERY day! XXOO

Dale - Thanks, Linda. I was just saying to someone else in Angie's 'circle' that she has attracted such a group of like-minded people to herself in this lifetime - the list goes on way beyond my capacity to name them all. We are all grateful (or should be) that she has brought us together.

Samantha J. - Beautifully written and shared Dale. You are such a remarkable person and I'm so glad I got to share a small part of your journey on this Earth.

Suzanne W. - We are so blessed to have you as friends & neighbors! Time flies! So happy for you to be able to share in the joy of a new baby girl in your life! Thank you for sharing your journey with us, I will never forget it! You've blessed us more than you can know! God bless you always!

Chalane H. - Love you.

Kimberly M. - We love you so much & am so thankful for your friendship & guidance in life. Baby will be lucky to meet you this summer - I can't wait for her to experience your magical ways. I would so appreciate a letter from you to her so she has a sense of you physically later on in life to go back to & read. Only if you felt inspired to do so though. Talk with you soon. So much love from all three of us.

Daisy S. - Lovely thoughts from a beautiful mind.

Jacki D. - Such a beautiful mind is right.

Holly S. - You're so brave and inspiring Dale, I feel like I know you so well, even though we have only met a few times. I remember the first time I heard Angie speak of you, and I could almost hear her heart race through the phone. I think she loved you the moment she met you. You brought such completeness to her life, you were her missing link. Not everyone has the chance in life to have a connection like the one you and her shared, no matter how long it lasts in this life time, it's rare.

Jennifer S. - Love you! I am so grateful for your friendship, thank you!!!!

Linda S. - Thank you Dale.

Dale - April 27 - 30, 2016

Today (4/27) is the four month anniversary of my diagnosis. If enough people ask me the same question enough times, it seems that I must eventually hear the energy underneath my answer enough to realize that I am lying to my questioner, and maybe even to myself, about the answer that I have been giving. And if I have been lying to myself for 4 months about the answer, this must be a pretty big deal for me to want to hide it for this long. A friend noticed the tone of my posts and asked an awkward question in an awkward way about an awkward subject (after all, what are friends for?) that has put me back on track (I believe). I have been getting the same message over and over for the last four months – look inside yourself for the answer. The more I ignored the feeling I was hiding about my answer, the more I hid the answer, and the feelings about the answer, until it seems that so many of my very closest friends were aware of the problem that I was oblivious to, and I was beginning to demonstrate subtle (to me) hints of a hidden rage that finally was brought to my attention in that awkward moment today. So here, only four months behind "schedule", I can finally face the root of the dis-function that could take me out before I am truly done here – rage at my father that I have not wanted to face, and that I have not wanted to forgive. Said this before, and thought I was past it and done, but I realize now it was only one layer, not the whole thing, and so I have a bit more work to do. It's also interesting, because there is a separation here of two people who love me, and what I see is that they are both right which is very cool to understand. It becomes hard to "judge" between them, because one has a lot more invested in the relationship than the other does, so when I can see that I don't have to choose, I feel a lot better about all of it.

Today was extremely interesting, as friends came down from a long way away to visit. These are friends that have been part of Angie's life for a long time, and we have renewed that friendship and extended it to include me in a meaningful way over the past few years, having annual visits here since our wedding. It is amazing how we can have relationships that are deep and meaningful, and that grow in the way that our spiritual lives grow, and yet it seems so organic that it is almost effortless. In this case, I'm talking about Rod and Tammy, and how many parallels there are in our lives, how much we have learned from them and their growth, and how much more we'd like to share with them over the time to come. Thanking the universe at 1:00 on a Sunday morning for all that she has to offer us.

Physically, I woke up 15 or 20 minutes ago from some kind of dream that I saw a perfect document in front of me that described exactly what was happening for me and what was going on within my body. It looked like a fully edited PDF with no errors and/or omissions, and yet I was not able to read it at all beyond that fact. I wonder if that is a result of the injection that Angie gave me at 10:30 last night, so that I could sleep through the night? I started to say earlier that this had been an interesting day, what with the visit and all. We had a normal morning, except that Angie had to spend some time getting ready for company on top of all of the normal stuff she does, which seems to always happen no matter how close the company is to our hearts. I spent my time more usefully than normal, reviewing all of the legal documents relating to the closing of our business, so at least I felt like I was making a contribution, and we got almost all of that dealt with. There are no impediments that we can see to the conclusion of business, as all of the issues seem to be related to minor things like typos and address issues, so that is a huge relief. Whenever legal rears its head, there is always the fear that something will be problematic, but in this case it just hasn't been so. I believe that is because the person we are dealing with (Tiiu McLim) is "one of our tribe" even though we have only just recently gotten to know her. Anyway, we got the legal documents reviewed, and I believe that they will all be finalized today or tomorrow, as there are no obstacles that we can see.

Rod and Tammie arrived early in the afternoon, and we were able to visit in the house for a bit, and then we were able to continue the visit outside with our horses and a fire in the wonderful fireplace area we have on the south side of the house. Even though I had to put Rod to work splitting wood and installing the pump for the waterfall (see what happens when you come to visit us now?), I was able to enjoy our space out there, and I truly believe that everyone else was as well. The horses entertained us all with a Code 3 Moose Alert, amongst other shenanigans, and we were able to discuss the many similarities in our lives which outwardly might seem quite different. I would really love to be able to get up to their place this summer, and will make sure that that event is at least on the wish-list.

Sadly, I don't remember too much else about the day as that was my limit for excitement, and I spent the evening snoozing and the night (until 1:00) sleeping, but I trust that the three had an enjoyable time with what was left of the day. Today they will head home while Angie and Deb will attempt a 25 mile ride in the Blackfoot. My mom, sister and brother-in-law are coming out to keep me company (I should be well-rested now) and we will drive out to the Blackfoot to spend the ½ way intermission with Angie and Deb, and if all is equal we will wait back at the house for them to finish the ride while I have some more quality visit time. My life truly is blessed with friends and family such as we have. I love that I am getting to know Angie's brother Peter better, maybe I'll stick around long enough to really get to know him in person. We've also had so many messages and phone calls from all of our other friends, neighbors and relations and I want to thank you all over again for being so understanding of our needs as well as your own desires for connection and relationship. Love to all of you.

Dale – Private message to Peter (Angie's half-brother from Austria) –

My brother from so many perspectives. I feel so connected to you, and yet we have never met. Is it possible that Angie pulls into her life all of these people who embody a certain type of energy, and in so doing creates a magical community of personalities who otherwise might not have been connected in this lifetime? Our Angie is the most uncommon of common denominators. I am so sorry to hear of your issues that are so similar to mine, and yet you are doing so well! Know that, no matter what, my heart reaches out to you, and I wish we were sitting down and sharing some of Ybb's finest beverages while we discussed our "troubles". No matter what the doctors say, I know that it is still possible that we will touch glasses before we are done in this life. Let me know if some of the things I express here are not clear, please.

Angie

Thinking back to the difference of opinion that a friend and I had regarding Dale and the "tone" of his posts, it comes back to a difference in perception so how can anyone be wrong? You perceive things the way you will and then you can re-evaluate, if you desire, but you cannot change what the other person perceived much less think of it as wrong.

I would have to agree that after finding out that the tumour had grown things most definitely did change. And so, perhaps the tone of the posts changed as well.

Also, after the fact, it was drawn to my attention (by an outside party) that the dream that Dale had about the "perfect document" might have been connected to this book!

This tattoo concept was designed for Dale by a client.

Dale - May 1 - 04, 2016

This has been the best weekend for quite some time, and in spite of the pain I experienced yesterday I would say it was definitely worth it. We had the most wonderful company from Thursday night all the way through last night in five different sets, nobody overstayed their welcome and every single person was a pleasure and a support to us. I spent a fair amount of time outdoors, we had fires in the regulation fireplaces to prevent any danger, and we were able to get the pump in the waterfall and get that going (what a pleasure to sit and just hear the water running), Angie and Deb rode in the Blackfoot and I was able to go and see them at the trailer between loops courtesy of my family, we went on a family drive to Mom's Ice Cream in Tofield (courtesy of none other than Mom). I finally feel like we got the drug regimen set up properly, and I have enough pain relief to keep me functional without being catatonic. That is so important to know where the line is, now I don't have to ask for extra drugs and so I won't have to have all kinds of drugs around that I don't need. The only downside was the puking and pain on Monday, which we are still trying to figure out the cause of, but I have to ask if I am willing to suffer for one day, if I have to, to have four really good days in return.

I think this brings us back to the big question, which is the simple and eternal (in human terms only) "What is the meaning of life?" Life is a card game. You are dealt cards, and you play the hand(s) you are dealt. Sometimes you fold ('life is too hard' or it's a strategy to set up the next hand), sometimes you bluff, sometimes you play a hand cautious, sometimes you play wide open (go all in), but you are dealt what you are dealt every hand. If you are fortunate, and you are trying, you learn more about the game with every hand, and you can become a master of the game (like "Gamemaster" by Robert Jacoby), and if you really get it, you can "Awaken" or even achieve Enlightenment. Just try to remember that every word is a collection of symbols that holds a whole pile of meaning that may not be the same for you as it is for everyone else around you. Try to see the meaning behind the symbols, in a 'softened' manner, so that you can take meaning from words and actions without taking much in the way of offence. If I can find a hint of LOVE behind every symbol, in the end my life will be FILLED with positivity.

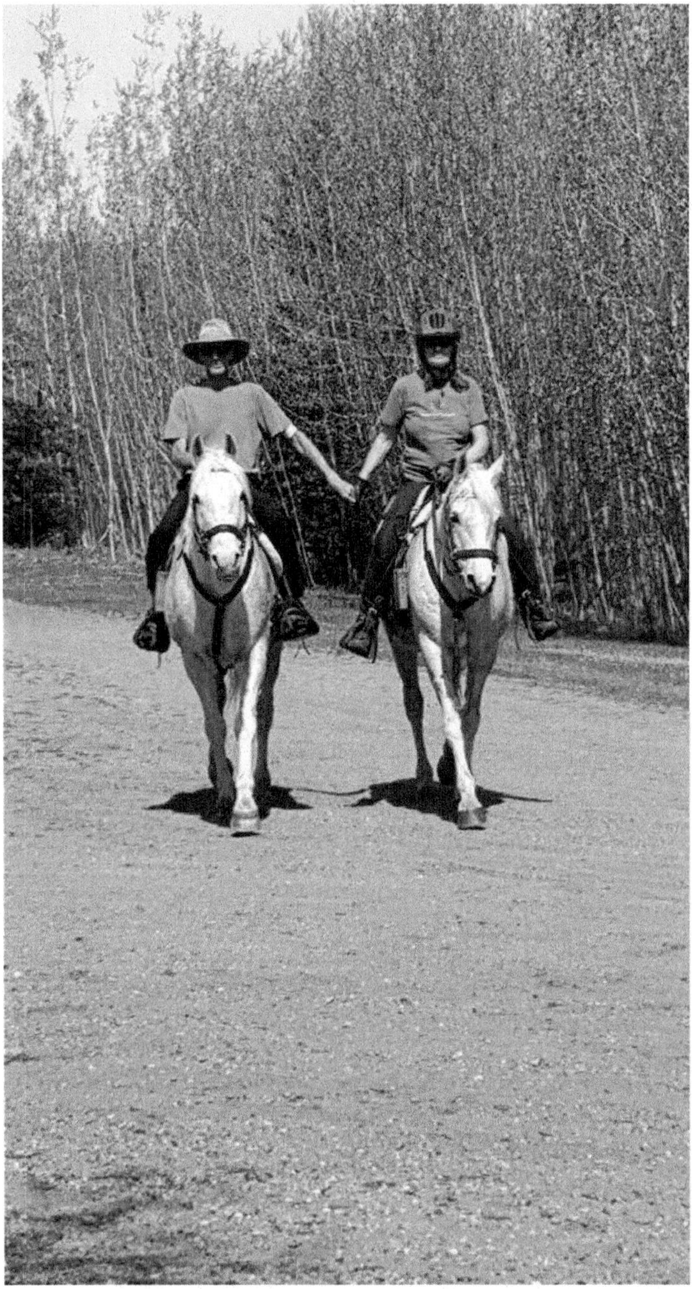

Dale was able to enjoy one last ride on Mo, in the parking lot at the Blackfoot Grazing Reserve.

Angie - May 4, 2016 - posted on Facebook

What started off as a pretty good day with Dale eating more than he has been, did not last. Dale had a really tough time tonight (I'll spare you the details) and he's getting weaker and weaker. He is brave and his spirit is willing but there's only so much the body can take. In the meantime we got the news that two people who are very close to us are in a very similar situation. I say enough already, I am strong but I am tired too. And, I'm not looking forward to the next stage.

Dale - May 6, 2016

Laura's (Dale's sister) birthday, May 5. I phoned her yesterday morning and told her it was her birthday, and it felt good. I believe her surprise was not that it was her birthday, but rather that I had phoned her myself and wished her a happy birthday – it's probably the first time in our adult lives that I have called on her birthday.

This week we got all the business stuff taken care of. Angie got the papers transferred between us, Tiiu, and the lawyer and that is finally all settled. As always, it seems, most of the issues are mere communications glitches, as there were absolutely no problems whatsoever with principals. Angie also got the Telus bill sorted out, and ongoing billing will now reflect the actuality of no business phones at the ranch from May 6 onward, and no cell phone for Dale past May 31.

Jen D. - Yesterday at 9:17am ...I've been thinking about the term, "vertical convection", it was mentioned in regards to how the fire "jumped" across the river. Every mean, hurtful, disheartening, angry, evil, hate spreading, blame throwing, statement regarding this situation is exactly that. It starts small and human nature "convects" it into a bigger more terrible, horrible matter. My ex is still up there, he's hopeful to fly out today...believe me, my heart is struggling on whether or not I give a shit. But my children do. And my heart needs help. Nothing is ever solved by blame. Ever. I've appreciated the videos of sheer kindness, compassion, help, problem solving, elevating fears, humanity reaching out. Inside every human is the ability to either convect bad, or convect good. Watch your mind, your tongue, your heart, your thoughts. We will be held accountable...for whatever comes out.

Dale - May 07, 2016

Angie has been plowing through the paperwork like there is no tomorrow, and it has been marvelous to see how much she has gotten done in terms of straightening everything out for us in the last few weeks. In the meantime, I have been getting the rest of my affairs in order (the things that Angie cannot do for me), as we have both accepted the probability of my imminent passing. As we solve the paperwork problems, and the spiritual and emotional questions, we are closer and closer to realizing that we are merely "moments" away from the event we have been anticipating since the end of December, and I want to take this opportunity to thank every one of you who has been in communication with us over the past months, and to assure you who still feel like you are not finished with all that "should" be said. There will not likely be a separate "celebration of life" ceremony after my passing – that is what we have been doing for the time we have had since December 28th, and we see no need to string it out even longer. While Angie will, I am sure, appreciate the support of her friends in the coming times, a specific time and place of "comforting" will not support her as she moves forward. If you have something that you want to say to us, email, card, letter, message, or somehow get it out now if you want us to know.

Yesterday, Roy and Marlene came up from Ponoka, and Roy did a bunch of my chores with Angie while Marlene "baby-sat" me. That worked out nicely, as there were a few things needing done that I just could not get up the energy for, and Angie did not have the strength for, and it gave us an excuse to spend time with dear friends – a nice doubling up of our time on several different fronts. This afternoon, Linda and mom came and sat with me while Angie got a ride in, and that also gave me some nice quiet family time while Angie got her mental health break. Both visits entailed some time in the sun with co-operating weather and cool beverages. Then a few more short visits and perhaps a chance to catch up with some friends we don't see a lot of – all in all not frantic but well planned. Next week will bring what next week will bring – the sun will come up Monday morning, and I will rise with it or not.

Angie

The decision not to have a "celebration of life" or anything similar, by any other name, was one we came to together. But in all honesty it was mostly made for my sake. There were over 400 people at Cody's celebration. I had spent a week preparing a slideshow to commemorate his life, this was at times gut wrenching, and it was also therapeutic. It's actually very much like going back through these posts (I had a difficult time getting to sleep last night and then woke up at 5:00 AM and could not get back to sleep). I had prepared it to end the slideshow on a good note, Cody surfing behind his beloved boat, downing a Twisted Tea with "We're here for a good time, not a long time" playing in the background. It ended with Cody slowly slipping down into the water. It felt appropriate and it felt relatively good, as good as possible anyway.

Afterwards the people in attendance wanted to offer their condolences and I wanted to honour each and every one of them for coming. This went on for over 2 hours without a pause or a moment to collect myself and it totally drained me emotionally. I am glad that I was able to honour all of those people but I simply could not imagine going through that again. And as far as that goes, I did not want to do another slideshow, plan music, or anything. Cody went suddenly without any warning. Dale's situation was completely different, he was publicly posting his deepest thoughts and feelings… for a very long time. People had ample opportunity to pay their respects while he was still here. What more was needed?

We often talked about how the circumstances were so opposite. In Cody's case the Facebook responses to his passing were incredible. I had no idea how well respected, loved and admired he was. I think he wasn't aware at all of the magnitude of adoration. He had NO opportunity to give any last thoughts or tell anyone what he might have liked to. Dale got to say it all and he got to hear and experience that love and admiration. What a wonderful gift to receive at the end of your life!

As far as my experience goes, as hard and shocking as it was to lose Cody so suddenly, it was actually much easier than watching Dale deteriorate as he did. It was fine for the first three months when we still had hope but it became more and more difficult as time passed.

Brittany H. - I just want to say I have never met you but my heart goes out to you and Angie I am so blessed that you're so strong and are such a great man to Angie! I wish there was a way I could make it all go away for you!!! I pray for you lots! It's not over Dale!!! The lord has you! I send you a hug and KEEP STRONG!!!! You're such a good role model for people like myself that are weak sometimes.... But my heart goes out to you both....

Hedi K. - Dale and Angie, Bob and I just want you to know that you are in our thoughts. Your sharing of your last few months has made so many of us stop and think about many things. I know my short journey with cancer brought me an awareness I had never had..... and appreciate the reminder that you have given me. Bob was reading one of your posts and said, "I can see why Angie loves the guy. I would never be able to be that brave." Take care and hope the next while is filled with peace and love.

Angie

Thank you Hedi and Bob. We are so glad that there was value in it for others. We both benefited from its creation as well. I may even make the whole thing into a book if it is able to help people that are going through this. Our home care nurse told us that the stats for cancer are now 1 in 2.2, that's crazy! It tells me that "they" don't really want a cure, this is big business. Anyway we are taking life one moment at a time and enjoying it. I wish you both peace and love too, there doesn't need to be a crisis for that to apply.

Patti B. - Sending you love, Dale. Thank you for everything.

Kat I. - Thank you Dale and Angie for inviting me to your celebration, for sharing a most intimate part of your lives. I, like others are at a loss for words. I feel as if you have been taking the lead in your journey and all I can say is "thank you".

Dale - You are more than welcome, Kat. I also have a new appreciation for the perspective I have seen from you in the last year or so - your wisdom and calming approach to so many things we have seen posted on Facebook makes me wish I had spent more time getting to know you in the opportunities we had.

Kat I. - likewise.

Tiffany T. - Love u guys Angie and Dale

Carol L. - I am recalling happy times with you Dale. You were a constant part of my life when I was married to Harry. Lots of fun times! Thank you for sharing your journey home. I look forward to continuing our relationship in the next life. May you will be filled with peace, love and contentment always.

Laurie L. - Hugs Dale! And thank you for being so lovely with me when we took those classes together in Victoria.

Katrin S. - Thinking of you as I am still on the river. I am so thankful that we took that class in CA together.

Jen D. -That means that I should come see u...I've been thinking about it for awhile. I'd rather see u living lol.

Trisha A. - I am also at a loss for words. All I can say is I admire you for doing things the way you wanted on your journey. You are a strong person and will be missed. May the rest of your time be filled with love and comfort.

Sarah C. - Thank you for sharing your journey with us all. Your strength is an inspiration to me and many others. Blessings to you and Angie.

Jennifer S. - Love you!!!!!!! Big big hug! I am so grateful to know you Dale. You are a courageous spirit and a wise man. May you have a peaceful journey. I am going to miss you very much and your posts. Sending so much Love to you and Angie!!!!!!

Lisa S. - You are the best Dale! Thanks for sharing and ALL the wisdom and caring you have given me! Sending prayers and love your way.

Chalane H. - Love, admiration, and blessings to you and Angie. I will be strumming my guitar, and singing some tunes in my church home...acoustics in there are beautiful. As time's meaning falls away I'll be holding you in my heart.

Cindy C. - Hugs and prayers to you both.

Cheryl P. - There are just no words that are enough. I try to bring it all together to share what you both mean... So in the moment: Your journey and words of wisdom brought me thru an unbelievably hard pregnancy, whatever you shared for the day always focused me for how I was dealing with my pregnancy...now I have a new little life and I struggle how to tell you goodbye... So I will stick with your message from the other day: love. And I know that when I have my message ready with EVERYTHING I want to say to you, even if it's only Angie I share it with it will reach you and that will be enough. And I feel strange putting it on Facebook, but your courage in sharing your journey here allows me to feel confident that it will reach you in the spirit and intent with which it is sent.

Aum S. - Thank you Dale for taking this time to share your journey. My heart hurts a little as I feel you preparing to depart this physical body. I celebrate you now and wish you many blessings on your next journey.

Anita G. - I am so grateful to creation that you are a part of my life's journey. Love to you always

Kathy N. - Thank you Dale for all that you have shared with us through your journey. I feel so blessed to have met you. You are a man of strength, and courage. May peace and comfort be with you. Love and hugs to you and Angie.

Wanda S. - Love your bravery, love your peace, blessings to you and Angie for sharing this amazing journey with us, praying for you both.

Jacki D. - Thinking of you Dale & Angie.

Suzanne W. - Dale I also want to thank you for sharing your journey, I realize that it's a really tough one. I admire your courage and perseverance and you will be missed. I'm sure we will reconnect someday. As you mentioned you may or may not see Monday morning, that certainly applies to all of us, by God's grace you and all of us will see Monday and many more days to come. Send you much LOVE & the BIGGEST HUGS you can handle. Peace be with you! God bless you and Angie. Love always!

Dee C. - God bless.

Lenka L. - Such courage in your words and actions. I bow to both of you with a lot of love in my heart and know that I will always remember you there. Love and blessings to you both!

Corina M. - Thank you for sharing your journey. I am in awe of your courage. Sending love to both of you.

Daisy S. - Hi Dale. I sat down on the floor tonight & read some old things I'd written when we met so many years ago. With all of the arrogance of youth (and we were so, so young, 22 and 23?) I wrote that I was one of your keys. And certainly you are one of mine. And I wrote down something you said that we laughed about then, "great minds think alike regardless of the facts!" I think it will still make you smile. There are gorgeous northern lights moving across the sky tonight. It reminded me of a lovely quote, "I have loved the stars too fondly to be fearful of the night." Love and peace and hugs to you and to Angie.

Terrence P. - I so wish there was a touch that could happen here. The words just are so inadequate. Suffice to say that this short time of connection we've had holds great value for me. I love you, Dale.

Sandra C. - Your journey puts it all in perspective, thank you for your courage in sharing it with us. I'll message Angie separately, but hope she makes that trip to the mountains with your spirit's blessing. Namaste and much love.

Dale S. - Well Dale, I've been thinking and praying for both of you lots during this time! I remember warmly our various conversations on so many diverse topics over the years. Thanks for all the kindness you have shown me and others over our Augustana Campus days. It has been very meaningful to discover all the mutual friends that I hadn't known were mutual until subtle comments here and there brought the connection to light! Well, whatever happens whenever, I trust our spiritual selves will continue being connected in some capacity until the end of time! And so I am wishing you an amazing abundance of deep-hearted moments in these potentially last physical days, my friend! Love you lots and forever, Dale S.

Lynn G. - Dale, although I haven't seen you for many years you will always hold a special place in my heart. I remember the first time I saw you - at Doreen's place in Coombs for a Jin Shin Do course. I drove up and you immediately asked if I needed help with my massage table. That's just the kind of guy you are: considerate and so willing to lend a hand. I have very fond memories of joy and laughter with you and helping you study for a big Jin Shin Do exam. I celebrate that you met Angie and have had such a beautiful life together. I will always remember you! Thank you for making such a positive difference in so many lives!

Cristina T. - Thank you for sharing your Journey. I am so honored to have met you and keep good memories. Remember how scared I was and you were so curious (about our shared ghost experience). For you it was such a natural phenomenon. Sharing your journey has helped me to be with it in acceptance of the eventuality of my own passing one day. Aren't we all here to go one day? Thank you once again. Love you Dale.

Dale - May 8, 2016

Woke up at 2:20 this AM and no idea why or what is going on. Some mild distress, got up to pee, Angie woke up, peed, showed me the Northern Lights, and they were beautiful and really moving. Watched the lights for a while, took a pain med (half dose), and laid back down. Hallucinated that I was a Chinese coolie for a while, lying on my back in a tunnel looking up through a pin-hole of light, wanting to back out of the tunnel but afraid of losing the pin-hole of light/air. I wonder if that was my potential to be reborn into my next incarnation, and if I was just not quite ready yet? I always thought I'd have a little time to process the last life before I had to choose a new one! Unless, of course, there is the possibility that I have "pre-selected" a series of lives/events much like the sport-select lottery idea. Ugh, I hope not!

I never thought I was asleep but now it's after 4:30 so I must have been. Stomach is gurgling and chugging, wind has been blowing for the last couple of hours, so I'm not sure what is going on. I wonder if this is the process of dying, or just the body speaking to me as the day begins – it is all very confusing. Remembering random people from my past, and then realizing why: Danny S. was looking at my Eagles songbook the other day, Gail G.'s name is on the inside cover – I rented her house on Garden Crescent in Calgary in the early 80's, bought a Yamaki 12 string acoustic guitar and later sold it to Phil F. as a gift for Gail, who also loved the guitar back in those days. Haven't seen or heard from them since the mid 80's in Red Deer, but remembered sitting at the table with them and their daughter/children the last time I saw them.

I cannot figure out if I am disappointed or discouraged by how long it appears to be taking to die. I really expected to be gone already, and yet I don't know what the hurry is. I still think the main push for me is not to be a burden for Angie, even though I know she's not in a rush to be "rid" of me. The hardest time is when I'm awake as my sky outside my window begins to lighten – what does the day hold? No job, no tasks, not much to hang onto. Worst thoughts of all – what if Angie breaks down before me? Worst because that feels so unutterably selfish, and yet it is definitely a present fear. We'll have to talk about that a bit today, I think. Census people came yesterday, and I just found out that Angie left their papers on the back of the Cobalt yesterday, so they are probably somewhere in Hay Lakes by now. Do you still have to fill out census forms if God blows away the forms? She couldn't fill them out until May 10 in any case, so now I guess she'll have to do the online version once she knows how many people actually live here May 10. Personally, I think it's hilarious because I've always been anti-census, while Angie has always been pro-census.

Guy T. - Just found you on FB day or two ago - I have a pretty light presence, but it occurred to me that you might be active, as a former tech head turned groovy hippy. And then I noticed you've been quite active recently, so I thought I would contact you. There's a nice picture of my girls from today, complete with sarcastic commentary that confused a friend and former neighbour - and a few glimpses into my rebuilt and reshaped life. You sound good, and like you've found peace with the cancer and bodily mortality. Enjoy the time you have left here; I've been thinking of you often, and appreciated your posts and insights. Several different cancers took my dad just over 15 years ago, on a beautiful spring day. He was able to reach out to his damaged family, and I had tremendous healing from the last few months of his life. But he never found peace with what was happening to his body, so I've admired how you came to terms with it - and know it was probably harder than it seemed from what you wrote. Don't worry if you don't have the time or energy to write back. Be in the moment with Angie and the friends who are coming through, and bask in their love. You've touched many people, and I'm so glad I got to know you, your sarcastic tongue, and quick, often inappropriate, wit. Go well, my friend.

Marion T. - Dale, It has been very difficult for me to know what to say to you and Angie. I'm still not too sure what to say but I don't want to wait any longer. I want to thank you for all your patience with me. You are not just a massage therapist or whatever hat you were wearing. All I do know is that energy flowed and things have come to the surface just as you said they would. I was hoping to work through them with you but you need to work through your own spirituality and I hope that you can before the end. I don't know where I'm going to find another like you. You are one of a kind and I thank you for everything you have taught you. Although you have not heard from me, I think of you and Angie and what you are going through every day. Angie, please know that I think of you always, but don't know how to express my feelings. Please note that I sympathize with you both. I would love to be there for you but am not sure how. Please come for tea and chat anytime you wish. Our thoughts are with you always. Marion and Harry.

Mary-Anne S. - Dale, I SO enjoy reading your posts...you speak of true unadulterated thoughts and feelings, I like that, somewhat entertaining and also eye opening as well, your insights are interesting, wish all the world would be more like this of speaking truths, be such a better place. Hugs to You.

Dale - I like to think that I have come to speak in a way that was considered quite normal for people say at the turn of the 19th century. I don't know if that is a romantic viewpoint, but I think I'll keep it anyway. Part of the "code of the West" that makes sense to me.

Pam B. - Your comment about taking so long to die is interesting. My dad said the same thing after he had been diagnosed as terminal. He was sure one day that that was it. He was going to be leaving this place that day. He had no real reason why he felt that way. He went on to live about another two years which was not necessarily a good thing.

Dale - Thank you for sharing that. My intention of course is to not stay past that point where it is not so good. I wonder if a person can just "will themselves to die" when a certain point is reached? Could be an interesting experiment.

Pam B. - I absolutely believe that people can will it Dale. My mom had a heart attack about 40 years ago. It was on a Saturday and she went to the hospital. She seemed to be doing good but was talking about who she wanted to have what. Of course I told her to stop it and that she was going to be fine. The dr. had her scheduled for a pace maker and then she would live a normal life. On the Tues. before they had a chance to do this, she had another attack. In the midst of it she looked right at the Dr. and told him not to try too hard. She did not survive this one. At the time they did autopsies on most people and they told us there was absolutely no reason that she should have died. For some reason she just gave up. You also hear the opposite. I know people that there is no way they should still be alive but they are. Because they want to be. With your attitude, I'm not taking any bets on you leaving this earth too soon.

Dale - Don't bet against it either Pam because there are many good and valid reasons to be ready to go at any time.

Angie

Dale's greatest concern through it all was MY wellbeing, both emotionally and physically. He could see how difficult it was for me on a day-to-day basis. I am transparent at the best of times, much less at the worst of times and the stress was taking its toll on me. As he said, I was not ready to be "rid" of him but I'd had enough of the situation alright. Those of you in our age bracket will remember the old saying "I'm not your nursemaid!" and those that don't should understand it to mean, I'm not here to look after your every whim and need. This of course is usually said in other circumstances, such as in the heat of the moment when a wife feels taken advantage of (usually a situation she's created herself). And I guess the reason I mention it, is that it certainly does feel like "enough already" when someone, even when you love them to the moon and back, relies on you for EVERYTHING! The choice to look after someone at home rather than sending them to a hospice or other facility is a HUGE responsibility and should not be taken lightly. I can see where, in many cases, relationships suffer greatly from the stress. I will say that by having Dale at home I was able to deal with daily chores and have a semblance of normal life that would've been difficult if I'd been going back and forth to visit him. And for Dale, I think it meant the world to him and for that reason alone it was more than worthwhile. Ultimately, it is the gift of love that is most meaningful.

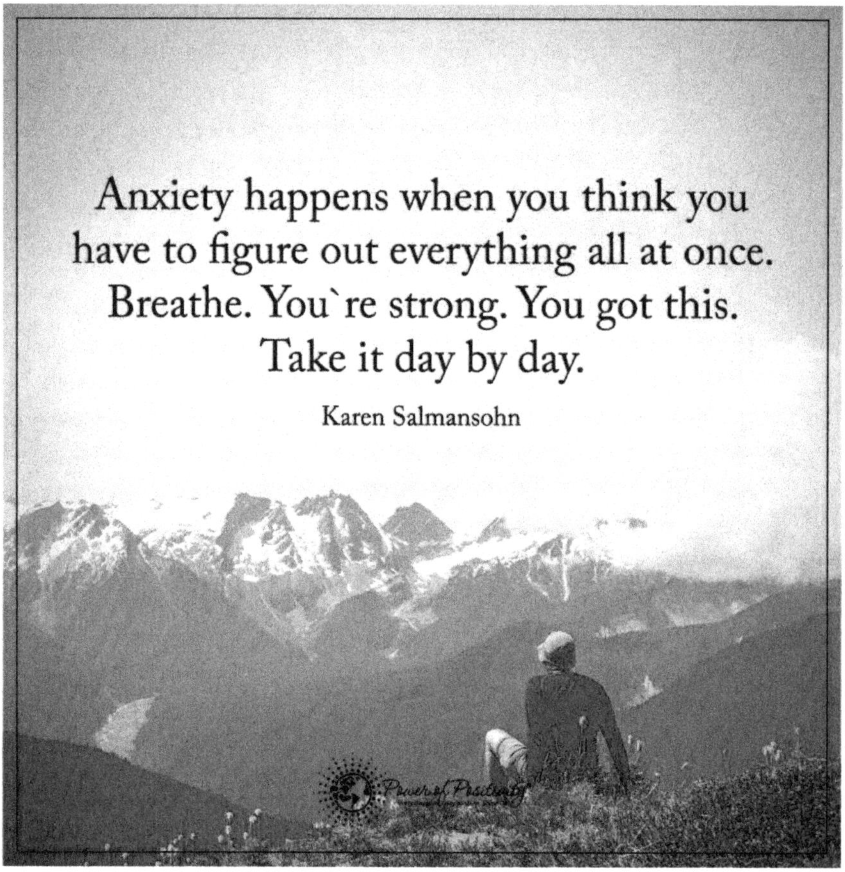
Anxiety happens when you think you have to figure out everything all at once. Breathe. You`re strong. You got this. Take it day by day.
Karen Salmansohn

Dale - May 9 - 10, 2016

Had a few visits Sunday, and some phone calls as well, that really brought things closer to home for Angie and me. First thing is I was completely rejected by the Alberta Educational and Medical Systems. All I wanted to do was to have my body used for medical advancement in some way – cadaver lab, cancer research, organ donation, even drug testing, but apparently once I've got this type of cancer my complete carcass is useless to the system. Ah, well. Now I can at least go shopping for the pine box to be burnt in, and we can plan together for an urn to hold part of my ashes. On the other hand, we get to go back over my bucket list and pick out the places where Angie can have portions of my ashes spread, and so far that has been a lot of fun and there has been no Ninja training needed. So Far! In the preliminary survey, I found that many of the places that had the most profound effect on me were Albertan and Canadian! How's that for living in the right place? Of course a good portion of those were CTR/ERA sites as well!

Afterwards, we also had some more meaningful calls from people about what we have meant in their lives, and vice versa, and that has been both a comfort and in other cases a mild discomfort as we move through those energy fields. It is harder to say goodbye to some people than I ever thought it would, or even could, be. Monday, on the other hand, was a day of holding patterns for me while Angie closed up more of the business end of things. I am trying to maintain a certain head-space, with some success, and preparing myself for transition. Last night we watched an old VHS movie filmed in Italian with English subtitles, called "Life is Beautiful". As unlikely as it seems, this was a concentration camp movie from WW II that I would actually highly recommend, but anyway, it was just right for where our heads are at now.

Carol L. - Well Dale I must say I have never ever experienced anyone sharing their journey as you have! You have touched my heart deeply! Thank you so much for all that you have shared! You are selfless right until the end with wanting to donate your body etc. I am also happy to read that you are enjoying your life moment to moment as well as the simple pleasures that come with each moment.

Liss L. - I agree with Carol, I am grateful to have had this insight on your journey. You mean so much to me and I know it does no good to cry for you, but I don't know what my life would have been if I never met you. You have taught me so much in the few years I've had the pleasure of knowing and working with you. "I just don't do shit that makes me feel weird." - Dale said once.

*Kylah C. – Dale, I have been honoured to have known you, to have you as a teacher not only in the healing realm but also in life. I am grateful you have given us the opportunity to share this journey with us. Thank you for everything *hugs*.*

Matthew N. - You are both such brave souls Angie and Dale, and Sandra and my thoughts and hearts continue to be with you through these difficult days. Dale, your online journaling has been amazing, terrifying and heartwarming. It is clear that you have had some very difficult times in this journey, however equally clear that you and Angie have a special kind of love and devotion to each other which has helped you conquer those hard days. As your 'trail' family helps Angie go down the trail, I have no doubts that you will be watching over her. May you find freedom from your pain on the other side. My deepest respects. Matt

Celine R. - Wow this is eerie, amazing and heartbreaking at all the same time. I've been following you two as I remember meeting you at my first clinic two or three years ago now. For the journey it sounds, you guys have seemingly handled it with such grace and a special love for each other. I am at a loss for words but I wish you warm thoughts.

Linda S. – Dale, you can leave this world knowing you were loved by sooo many and that you have nurtured so many. You are a man with great strength and dignity. You have accomplished so much and touched so many and there are so many things you have done in my life that I thank you for and even though we missed a few years I have a lifetime of memories with you and more memories to be made with your beautiful wife. I will love her always. I will love you always. THANK YOU FOR BEING YOU...Linda

Michelle C. - I just finished painting a Thank you card for you, I will send it by mail today. I have attached it as well so we do not have to wait for delivery. I wanted to send you a note of Thanks for the gift of health that you have given my family. You brought my mom's vitality and mobility back, without you she may have never climbed the hills of Drumheller again. Thank you for the friendship with my father and care you have given him. Thank you for the strength you gave me before my surgery and the healing after treatment. I appreciate the nurture and love you have given my children helping them to grow tall and healthy over the years. My thoughts are with you and Angie today.

Angie

Since Dale's passing he has been spread over many of the places that we chose. He has been on many a trail ride, and deposited at finish lines, and other gorgeous locations.

Water colour painting done for Dale by Michelle.

Dale - May 11, 2016

So there is now a new ritual that takes place regularly. I open my eyes, then I find a clock, then I check the time, then I find my notebook and check the time of my last dose, then I do a quick calculation and whether it is night or day I call Angie if I am over four hours because that means I can have more. The game part of the ritual is to not be under four hours even by minutes, because that would be giving in to the pain and not good in the long term. (Ha! Ha!).

Another new experience today will be the "sick-sitter" (otherwise known as respite care, which does sound better). Someone that I don't know is going to come and sit with me for part of the day while Angie goes off and takes care of business. This will be good because then Angie won't have to worry about me falling down and getting hurt when no one is around to remedy the situation. Not that there is much chance of that, but then I don't really have a good track record of looking after myself. Having now met Leona, I feel much more at ease about having a stranger in the house. Today I got good news about the massage table from Shawn, he's got the paint and assembly planned, and is just ready to put the finishing touches together like switch mounts, and should be able to present the finished product tomorrow all ready to go. This feels a lot like Christmas, way to go Shawn!

Another happiness about tomorrow is that I am expecting Harry to visit, if all goes well. Hopefully I'll hear tonight, but if not I'm sure it will work out. I am amazed at how my perspective has changed over the last few months. A glass of cool, sparkling water is now almost as enticing as a nice cool beer was 6 months ago. A spoonful of ice cream with chilled peaches is now the ultimate dessert. A juicy piece of BBQ sausage, skin removed, with Dijon mustard is now the gourmet meal I crave. And a simple visit with a good friend is my most coveted appointment. Priorities. Have. Changed!

Angie

This would have been my father's 87th birthday. He lived in Switzerland where self-determination (assisted suicide) is legal, under meticulous guidelines. He suffered from emphysema and had been in severe pain for several months following bowel surgery to remove an obstruction. His quality of life was unbearable, therefore he chose to end his life on January 2, 2015.

It takes more courage
to let something go
than it does to hang on to it,
trying to make it better.
Letting go doesn't mean ignoring a situation.
Letting go means accepting what is,
exactly as it is, without fear,
resistance, or a struggle for control.

- Iyanla Vanzant

Dale - May 12, 2016

Today I'm still thinking about this photo I saw posted yesterday. It goes very well with the message I seem to be getting consistently, which is that Priorities. Have. Changed! And what a wonderful idea for all of us. When I think about how differently I see things today than I did six months ago, it is hard to believe that I am still the same person that I was back then, and yet all of the beliefs and patterns of today were already imprinted on me then, they just had not blossomed as they have recently. Plant those flowers, water them, fertilize them, and be patient. When the conditions are right, the crop will come in.

The tumour seems to be progressing in a slow and steady manner, so there is some pain and discomfort this morning that seems to be getting slowly stronger. That being said, meds every four hours are doing a pretty good job of managing except for the odd spike like this morning, where the discomfort has been enough to keep me awake without leaving me dysfunctional. I guess that is both my opportunity and my incentive to read and write, as the correspondence at least takes my mind away for a while. Not that I'm trying to avoid the body-mind connection, but rather that I want the message to not be shouted loudly and continuously in my ear. In the spaces between reading, and writing, I continue to work on forgiveness, and am still being surprised at the resentments I am finding.

Dale - May 13, 2016

I received a letter from my sister Laura yesterday morning. The first part of the letter was very touching, and helped me to understand myself a little better, and also some of the things that have been difficult for me to process in my life, how I have reacted to those things, and what I can do with those feelings left over from attempting to process those things. I would even say that The Letter, part I, was an instrument of healing and love, and that is exactly what I will use it for. I learned some things that I did not know, which helped to release some more of the resentment I had felt toward my dad as I processed the depth of the pain he must have felt, knowing that his relationship with his father was most likely as troubled as mine was with him, and even learning that he had gotten some resolution with his father that I never was offered (even if I would have accepted it). These seemingly conflicting directions were just tangled enough to help me release another layer, and that was very cathartic for me.

As I read further, I discovered bits in The Letter, part II, that helped me to clarify just how much my sister and I (and I believe many Christians and I) see the same events and attitudes from such diametrically opposed viewpoints that often what I view as dialogue is merely the throwing of "mud-balls" against each other's' castle walls. My sister seems to believe that the actions of people, or how they respond to their inner pain, can be blamed on external sources (like alcohol) while I believe firmly that the emotional pain is the stimulation for their actions and that emotional damage is what triggers all of the actions that will find a way to be expressed until the damage is healed or the life ends unhealed. In other words, I am saying that the person will continue to "act out" their emotional damage until they can see themselves that there is no value in spreading the damage to others, and that the only healing comes from the soul outward rather than from redress inwards. It seems to me that this can become a very subtle differentiation, and it is often missed as the real point of contention. To put this into simple words, the therefore alcohol does not "cause" the person to do bad things. What it does do is remove the inhibitions against doing hurtful things. The bottom line is that as long as my father was a 'wet' alcoholic, he had many redeeming features, and in spite of the pain I suffered, I actually liked him a lot more than I ever did once he became a 'dry' alcoholic. It seems that he tried harder to be part of my life, and I felt more connected to him and more like he was "real" when he was a drunk. I had a harder time reconciling the "good" father who took us to church and was actively involved in the church than I ever had with the drunk who sent us to church on Sundays while he slept in from Saturday night (I know, this is a huge over-simplification). My sister also commented on the "unbreakable bond" that happens when you are raised in the same household, and that is something that I also don't see as a given. Growing up in the same household only creates an unbreakable bond when mutual solace and comfort are also taken as a result of the ongoing traumas that are co-experienced. When the mutual traumas just result in more separation, there is only more separation experienced.

Then I got to The Letter, part III, and I begin to see the final disconnect. Because I do not proclaim Christ as my Saviour, and because I am still able to dig up (smaller and smaller) vestiges of the old anger, especially as I dig deeper and deeper into the tentacles that have moved these feelings into more remote nooks and crannies of my heart, body and mind, it is assumed that I have not forgiven my father. My assumption in all of this has always been that the Christian denominationally based faith just does not agree with me, and what Laura has gifted me here is a clearer vision of the real problem, which is that I believe I am experiencing a creational forgiveness rather than a blanket forgiveness provided by some other being. In other words, each step of my forgiveness process releases another block which allows another layer to release and bring me a much deeper "knowing" of the source of my feelings, so that I can also recognize these patterns building up and stop future creation of resentments long before they can become problematic. Rather than believing that we can expect change to come from external sources I believe it all comes from within – by willingness to open ourselves to experience the world, we also begin to actually see the potential for acceptance of change. Phew!

The letter –

Hi Dale, I just wanted to have a little talk with you before you go. I want you to know that I love you – that I have always loved you, because you are my big brother. Over the years I have often envied some of my friends who had (and have) a unique, soft and good relationship with their brothers – something that we never had. But I love you none the less. My first recollection of a memory is of you trying to hold my hand, and me pulling it away and wanting to do it (stand maybe?) on my own. This pattern followed through much of our childhood – you wanting to 'show me' something, and me wanting to do it my way. I think I still learned a lot from you – just because you were older and so did know more than me! I remember watching in awe as you practiced that 'Hawaiian guitar' as we called it – sliding that metal bar across the strings and making incredible music – I loved that sound. I remember trying to 'keep up' with you as we walked along Banning Street towards Sunday School – and then sitting beside you in church, because we both wanted to 'stay'. (probably to avoid whatever was happening at home, I think). I remember the time you locked Linda and I out of the house, not knowing we had the kitchen tap running into a closed sink – what a mess we had to clean up (before Mom and Dad got home). I remember your avid defense of us to the neighbors, and even as a child your stand against injustice (and favoritism). I remember your incredible ability to memorize Scripture – and the contests you had with others (Ron mostly I think) in reciting full chapters in church. I saw what went on in our house, through timid and scared eyes. I hid more than any of you other kids, went to friends' houses more, even hid in the bushes beside our house. I know that you took the brunt of Dad's irrational anger and suffered most at his verbal lashes. Here is what happened in my life… … … … … . I always had a special relationship with Grandpa Pierce, because I was born on his birthday! He always gave me a special gift on my birthday, and he was a soft, cuddly, and loveable grandpa, that filled a void in me. I don't know if you remember or not, but it was on Grandpa's deathbed, after his stroke, that he called for Dad, and had a chat with him… … … … .Dad never had a drink after that day. (and like it or not – it was Dad's drinking that made him the menace he was). I was 11 eleven years old and in later years made an unfair parallel between the loss of my Grandpa with the emergence of a different Dad. My heart became hard and heavy towards Dad as a result and I simply couldn't get past that sense of hurt in my heart. It was just before Mom and Dad's 50th anniversary celebration (which I never thought would happen), that I was struggling with what to say for a speech – and God healed my heart – God turned my heart of 'stone' into a heart of 'flesh' and I was able to get past the hurt and step into a new relationship based on love and forgiveness, with Dad. That experience totally changed 'me' - not Dad – and I am a different person today, because of that. God changed me! You and I have not been connected through our adult life. And I know, that the few times I have reached out to you – it has been to involve you in our lives in some way – usually planning something for Mom and Dad – and your response was always that, "I only contacted you, when I wanted something". That's true, because ultimately – that's what families are for - and I know that you are realizing that now, as you travel this end of your earthly journey – it's not ONLY families that support each other – you have many, many good friends that have supported you and Angie well through these past months, but the very base connection of our emergence into this world and growing and learning and growing up together in the same physical space creates an inevitable and unchangeable bond that cannot be erased by choice. You know my belief system – that God is the author of life and death – that Jesus paid the sacrifice for sin with His life on the cross, to redeem us to the Father. I have had times in my life too, where I wandered away from relationship with God, because of people, or circumstances, or wrongs, or injustice. But the day God healed my heart, was the day that the true meaning of that relationship kicked in and God has been my strength, my peace, my confidence, my life ever since. And having cancer, has caused me to re-evaluate the brevity of this earthly life and what is important in light of eternity. I know, beyond a doubt, that God is real, that heaven and hell are real, that we will all spend eternity in one of those two places and that we have the ability to choose which it will be. My heart hurts, to think that you have rejected God and heaven. My heart hurts, to think that you have not had the opportunity for God to manifest Himself in your life, on this earth, enough for you to trust Him with your future. I only ask that you invite God into your last days, and give Him a chance to change your mind about eternity. That is my hope and that is my prayer! I love you Dale - a piece of me will die when you depart this earth – just because – you're my brother! Laura Pierce.

Angie

I am grateful to Laura for giving me permission to publish her letter. It allows you readers to experience her perspective in the exact way that she expressed it.

Dale – Harry and Lori drove up from Calgary today to spend what may be (although nothing is guaranteed) one of the last opportunities we will have to spend time together in this life. As my oldest (I mean longest running – I believe our friendship dates back to 1956 at least) friend, I treasure any time that I get with Harry, and I feel like I married Lori about the same time that Harry did. I was there the night they met in Calgary, I was at their wedding in Winnipeg, and our lives have been loosely intertwined in all of the 30+ years between. My heart is filled with joy to see also how well Angie connects with Harry and Lori, and I trust the Universe to see that friendship continue in the manner that it has grown.

Finally, Shawn brought over the assembled electric massage table that he has been finishing for me. I was both overwhelmed in the most positive way possible at the marvelous job he did of finishing the table in a manner that would have made me proud to call this my work, and saddened by how totally drained I was, and therefore unable to convey truly how pleased I am with the outcome. This weekend we will post photos of the finished product and complete the job of re-homing my project that I started with Aron so long ago. Shawn, just so I am clear, I couldn't have been prouder of this table than I would be if I'd done it myself. You are a master craftsman. Thank you. Also thanks to Amy and the girls for dropping over – again I feel bad for not having the energy left to just enjoy you guys, but I'm afraid that all of my reserve tanks are just about bone dry, and my days of casual visiting may be done.

Today we are taking it completely easy, because I want to stay alive long enough to see Amanda Rheaume tonight.

Angie

I don't believe that Dale ever mentioned that Harry is his cousin. He considered him to be so much more than family.

Carol L. - Attention: Light Workers! An "In Transition" Story: I am deeply touched and forever changed by the writings of Dale Pierce as he posts daily journal writings on his Facebook page. He is making his exit in a way that a light worker would be proud to leave! He shares in his writings of how he has been working through healing his issues while he journeys on the road to the transition of ending his time in this body and moving onto his new life. His postings are public so I encourage you to read them! Here is a piece of the wisdom that he has shared: My sister commented on the "unbreakable bond" that happens when you are raised in the same household, and that is something that I also don't see as a given. Growing up in the same household only creates an unbreakable bond when mutual solace and comfort are also taken as a result of the ongoing traumas that are co-experienced. When the mutual traumas just result in more separation, there is only more separation experienced.

Dale - May 14, 2016

Last night was an amazing night. Angie looked awesome, and managed the evening's logistics like a professional, but neither of those things ever surprise me. Jean was looking at peace with life tonight too, that really suits her, and her energy was so good. Daisy continues to be as beautiful as always, both inside and out, and it was good to see Jason again after so many years. Rod and Tammie were in great form, as was Amanda and this is the first we've seen her with Anders and Anna as her backup. I even enjoyed David Gogo for a set, and that was awesome as well. I keep saying awesome, I guess that might be the word of the night. The reality, though, is that I think there are few ways this night could have been more perfect for me. Thank you to the best bunch of friends I could ask for (even those who could not be there in person last night were there in spirit).

Today has also been a good day – because I was careful about what I put in last night, I have not been suffering a backlash today and that is a relief. Last night I said goodbye to a few good friends, and today I also got to say goodbye to a few more good friends, and it pleases me to be able to spend a few minutes with each of some of the people who mean so much to me. First was Deb Clary, who has taken Mo under her wing and will get him up to competition shape if that is possible, and will take him as far as possible in any case. She cares about horses in a way that I was just learning to, and she has a lot of "horsemanship" knowledge that I never had, which makes her perfect for Mo, plus she is a good friend for Angie to ride endurance and CTR with. Thank you Deb for stepping up – my heart can relax.

I also had a moment to say goodbye to Doreen and Larry, even knowing that I may possibly see them again this week. Larry and Doreen started off as clients, but are the kind of people Angie and I would have loved no matter where or how we had met them. Some people come into our lives for a long time, and some people come into our lives for a shorter time, and as long as connections are made, we have to be satisfied with what we get. With Larry and Doreen, connections were made. Later this weekend I may get a bit of time with Shawn and to see the finished massage table, I'll probably also see Dennis and Mary-Lynn this weekend, and I may even be able to see Terry W. and Chris E. as well.

Bruce W. - Hey Dale. I know I haven't been a close friend over the years but it is a wonderful thing to have had you in my life since you moved into the neighbourhood. Darts, karaoke, riding and I seem to remember a dance or two we were both at, including our wedding. Know that you are loved and a very special guy. Currently I think I have a cold (either that or newly acquired allergies) so I don't want to subject you to that. Please know that my prayers for you are for peace and no pain. Judging by your posts I do believe you have peace. God bless and God speed.

Dale - Thanks Bruce. You're right, we haven't been close, but that does not mean we are not friends. And thanks for the consideration - I am trying to maintain the "healthiest dying man that we know" status. Feel free to call or to visit once you know you're not contagious. Bruce: Will do. Have a good night...

Dale - May 15, 2016

Well, I had a good night, pain management was successful, and here we are at Sunday Morning getting ready for a private concert on my back deck from one of my favorite but (I thought) least published local musicians. I have heard Terry on classical guitar, which I loved, and this morning I'm going to hear him on the electric piano. I never knew his talents had this many facets, but I am ready to enjoy this concert thoroughly. This is after the private concert now, and I have to say that I was deeply moved by the experience. We listened to Terry's repertoire of classical-jazz compositions and I think I can speak for both of us in saying they were deeply moving and evocative pieces, and I am so glad to have been gifted his private concert.

Enjoying our private outdoor concert.

I do not know what the rest of this day will bring – I find myself less and less connected to earthly events, and yet still strangely disconnected from higher events, and I can't help but wonder if that is merely because I really have no idea what to expect around this next corner. I wish that I had one of those milk-carton periscope thingies that we used to make as kids, only one that could see spiritually as well. I honestly thought that things would be simpler here, at this stage, or at the very least, clearer.

Dale - May 16, 2016

Had a visit with Dennis and Mary-Lynn in the afternoon, and then a quiet evening trying to come to peace with everything. It is becoming harder and harder to maintain equilibrium as this stretches out. Everyone close around me is trying so hard to be patient and loving, but I want this to be over with, already, and maybe I'm reading things in that are not there sometimes. The hydro-morphone surely does promote a wee bit of paranoia, at certain regular stages in the pain – no pain cycle. If you or a loved one is going through this, please recognize that sometimes it truly is the drugs doing the talking. The other thing I am coming to realize more and more is that there must still be something holding me here, in spite of how sure I think I am that I am ready to leave. I will dedicate the rest of my life to trying to figure out what that thing is, because I believe that might also help to shed some light on my mother's dilemma. She also feels like she'd like to be done with this world, but is being held here by something she does not understand.

I'm hoping to have another long chat with my sister Linda today, and maybe even with my mother as well. Depending on how the week goes, Angie may get to ride in the endurance race this Saturday in Winfield, which would please me hugely. I would truly like to see her on the way to her 1,000 mile buckle in distance riding before I go. Unfortunately, Mo is out of this event for sure because of what looks like a recurring left groin injury, and hopefully we will know in the next little while if that is going to be potentially fixable or not, after an assessment by Deb's therapist. I hope there is some potential for him, as it looks like Glory's "tiny" slip might have permanently put her out of contention as a distance horse, leaving Angie with no spares and a lot of equine liabilities. Interesting how we are seeing all these parallels between human and equine happening at the same time recently.

OK, so now it is late Monday morning, and Linda is going to come tomorrow with Mom instead, because the wind came up real strong today, and Angie and Deb have decided to try to wait until tomorrow to try to ride, in case it is calm enough that they can feel more comfortable riding in the bush tomorrow. Either way, I'm good, as that just gives me one more day to ponder the big questions I want to ask Linda and Mom. We've got a continuous but gentle flow of company coming and going and that just seems to work perfectly for us.

I think our friends are the best friends anywhere, and just to point out how marvelous even the absurdities are in our current situation, I want to tell you about the "shit-storm" that blew through here the other day. With all of this dry, windy weather we've been experiencing lately, Angie and I were sitting on the swing on our south 'viewing patio' between the apple trees, enjoying the warm sun and the breeze. At the south end of the property across the field we are facing is our 'indoor arena' which is merely a canvass covered area for riding in inclement weather, and the canvass started to rattle and shake in an odd manner, which caught our attention. Then as we watched, it seemed like a whirlpool of very dry horse turds, extremely light because of the heat and the wind, began to move very slowly from the arena straight towards us. This continued for a good five – ten minutes, until just before our view of the whirlpool was blocked by the lip of the rise leading up to the driveway fence, where the whirlpool revealed its true size as it picked up a bunch of straw rubble at the bottom of that hill, and we saw that it was actually a large 'dirt devil' about 30 feet high, and still moving on a direct line between the arena and the house, and as we continued to watch in semi-disbelief this dirt devil proceeded to dump its contents directly onto the swing we were sitting in, as we scrambled to throw a sheet over our heads to protect us from most of the debris. At no time in this "ordeal" had we felt in danger, and in fact due to the extremely dry conditions there were absolutely no injuries (except to our dignity) because everything that fell on us was extraordinarily light and dry, but the thing I remember most was the combination of disbelief and delight etched on Angie's face as the wall of debris hit us.

The calm after the "shit storm".

This is where the infamous "shit storm" happened. Too bad we didn't have a camera handy at the time when it happened.

Angie

Oh I do remember that "shit storm" so well, it puts the look of delight right back on my face just to think about it. In many ways it was like some of the things we endured on this journey.

Dale - May 17, 2016

Deb and Angie are out jockeying the truck and trailer around this afternoon, getting comfortable with the rig in our yard so there will be no problems on the coming weekend, so it is looking more and more like the whole thing is a done deal. It pleases me to see plans being made and life going on, because no matter what I believe life will go on throughout all of our dramas. I'm sitting up with a little cup of coffee (doesn't keep me awake at nights anymore, strangely) and enjoying their progress. I do a little meditating, think about what is happening to my body, do a little writing, talk to a friend in person, on the phone, by message or by email, and am content to wait and see what will be. I'm reminded of the Dustin Hoffmann movie, "Little Big Man" where Chief Dan George (I don't remember his character's name) says, with glee, "It is a good day to die!" I believe that every day is a good day to die. Or to live.

I am seeing that for me it is very important to have a presence in the house as I go through this process. I believe that a live person who I can talk to is the best, because at the very least there seems to be a want or a need to not be alone at this stage. In the night, when the air is dead calm, and the only thing I can hear is my own breath, the world just feels so empty that I wonder if other life does actually exist. Also, it is important for me, at least, to be able to bounce thoughts and memories off of other people as I go through all of the letting go that I want to be able to do in these end times.

I got a chance this afternoon to reaffirm both my existence and my troubleshooting skills as I was able to help Deb and Angie figure out what was wrong with the wiring on the battery power for the fifth wheel unit. Deb had caught and repaired the fried main fuse from the batteries into auxiliary power, but the rest of the wiring on her unit was done in a "unique" manner that made it hard to trouble-shoot the underlying problem. After hearing her description, it sounded to me like a main relay issue, and with a simple volt-meter a very simple problem to verify. Of course, in all of the confusion here, the meter was nowhere to be found but with a little luck and my obtuse desire to 'figure it out' we were eventually able to confirm the culprit. Fortunately, there was one available in a shop in Edmonton and Deb was able to zip in and pick it up today and we have until Friday morning to get it all installed and working properly for her (meaning she will install it with perhaps a little guidance from me, if needed). So now that problem should be resolved quite satisfactorily.

I had a real good talk with my mom this afternoon, as well, and I feel like I got some very satisfying information from her that helps me piece together the stuff I have felt with the information Laura was able to give me, and come to a much deeper understanding of my father than I have had in recent years. My mom tells me, in a manner that I believe, that my father loved me very much, and that he wanted to reconcile some things with me, but that circumstances conspired into leading him to believe he had more time than he did. Also, knowing where I was at the time, I know that I made it way harder for that to happen than it ever needed to be, so I can no longer allow myself in good conscience to blame him for the way things ended. So here it is, in public and from my heart – Dad, I forgive you for any pain you may have caused me, and I ask your forgiveness for any pain I may have caused you. I will accept that after all you loved me the best way you knew how to, and I will offer you the love that I have withheld most of my life. I promise to explore this as much as I can over the next days as I continue.

Suzanne W. - So beautiful! I am so happy for you to be able to come to this conclusion with the forgiveness of your father and yours as Well! My heart goes out to you! Sending you Big Hugs!

Terrence P. - heavy duty, Dale. I'm curious how that made you feel.

Dale - Hey, Terrence. What aspect of this are you inquiring about? Assuming that your interest is in fatherly love, I have felt a sense of peace around my feelings towards my father since I made the decision to be more open to love, but it has also brought me to an awareness of how judgemental I have been and potentially continue to be towards other people as well, in related matters. Thus another aspect of the cascade effect.

Patti B. - As a parent, I look back on all the ways I was a terrible parent and I'm filled with pain and remorse. I loved my son more than anything in the world and never wanted to cause him pain or make his life harder than life already is, and yet I did. I want a do-over. I want to raise him again with the knowledge, wisdom, life experience, and external supports I have now. And that's when I am able to forgive myself a little bit, when I look back with compassion and see that (in your words, Dale) I loved him the best way I knew how to, with all the deficits in knowledge, time, energy, outside supports, physical and mental health that I had at the time. I'm saying that I think I (and maybe many parents) can relate to your dad's failures to some extent. So, I am so happy and comforted to see, Dale, that you are able to forgive your dad all his failings toward you, and you are able to see that he loved you the best way he knew how to at the time. What a gift that your mom is still here to tell you some things you didn't know.

I want to add that I don't think it's always true that parents love the best way they know how to. Possibly, some parents are truly nasty, selfish people, undeserving of forgiveness for the horrible ways they treated their children. I don't know. I'm speaking only of my personal experience and how it might relate to yours. Thank you again for your openness at this time, Dale. It's helping so many people, including me.

Dale - Thank you so much Patti. I have come to the belief that there is nobody that is undeserving of forgiveness, when you know their whole story, and I hope you understand that I do not take that position lightly, as I have seen and been told of some pretty horrible things that have been done by parents.

Darlene K. - I hope you know how much I love you and always have! Sorry cousins, but Dale has always been one of my favorites!!

Dale with his sister, Linda and Mom, Helen.

Dale - May 18, 2016

Wow. Today has already been another day of catharsis, and it is only 9:30. Having my Mom and my sister here has brought me such peace of mind already that I can't help but imagine how many more wonderful things this day can bring. I have a much broader picture of how each of us allows pain to begin to close us to the wants and needs of others, and how my reaction to MY pain has allowed me to close to the wants and needs of my own family in a way that restricted their ability to heal, and to help me heal. I have been given the most wonderful gift of the time and patience to ferret out, one layer at a time, the clues, one building on the next questions to ask, that have finally given me an understanding of how my actions have directly and indirectly affected response in those around me. I even have an understanding of how my actions could create a cascade of effects either for opening or for closing from different points in the past, present, and future. Once I could see these potentials, it seems much easier to make choices, but for those who are interested, let me explain the mechanism that lead up to this point.

For years, and as of several days ago, I had a view of how my father had acted that was based on my memories of events and my sister Laura's additions that I received recently started to change all that. That bit of information, sent with a sister's love in the face of my rejection, allowed me to open a bit more to other possibilities in my understanding of what had occurred. Yesterday I was able to talk to my Mom about things that I had previously been closed to, and Mom was then able to let go of some of her closedness around past events, and give me more clues that she had not necessarily intended to release. None of these included intention to harm by withholding, but in retrospect it is much more obvious after the fact how that could have happened than it could have possibly seemed before. Then this morning, I was able to talk to my sister Linda about my Dad's death in a way that I had not been able to before, and I believe that happened because of the slightly more open attitude I was displaying to her, which reduced her fear over triggering unexpected reactions. Now some of the things that Mom told me make even more sense, and I'm even starting to understand my brother's reaction to all of this in a different way (not that I was having trouble with him at all, but rather that I didn't understand him). In short, Laura's 'defiant' act of openness inspired opening from Mom, Linda, and myself that all fed on each other and became an increasingly powerful cascade of openings. My hope is that the cascade continues into the future to include further openings and even more participants.

Terrence P. - Oh, what a tangled web.

Dale - Yes, that is the absolute truth. However, what a joy to be able to begin to understand the web, and to be able to follow the flow as it grows and leads one from one thought to another, each one building on the one before. The beauty and the power in this is to see how each little action, created to protect me or the person I am talking to at the time, has the potential to bring up the need for another layer of obfuscation to soften a blow that is only potentially harmful, and how we therefore cloud the issue unnecessarily based on what the other person 'might' be hearing. How much easier just to be able to speak plainly from the heart without the need to try to anticipate what might hurt the other!

Dale - Not posted on Facebook -

I'm not so sure I was fair to myself in taking all the blame for the above events, although my intentions under reference at the time of writing a letter to my parents were rather hurtfully aimed. I was hurting myself, and really looking for the same answers I had been looking for all my life – I wanted my Dad to say "I love you", and even if he did not say those three words to me, Linda tells me that she overheard him tell Jim that he loved me and forgave me for anything that I had done to hurt them. The fact that he didn't say it to my face in exactly the way *I might have demanded it* is probably not so important any more. I can just accept the fact that he said it as proof that the feeling was there.

Dale - May 19, 2016

Another thing that comes out of my Mom and sister's visit is just the idea that I'm talking about blame again. The big problem with blame is that as soon as we're talking about blame we are focusing on separation, which is really the big picture issue in all of this. Separation of each of us from the other, and separation of all of us from the eternal, from the divine, and from creation. Blame is just a way to anaesthetize my feelings so that I don't have to fully experience them, and if I don't feel them, I don't feel the guilt that comes with them. Forgiveness is the antidote to shame, and that is what we mostly seek in this life.

Last night the ladies from the Full Moon Society took a big bite out of the technology battle, and included Angie and I, and Larry, in their moon celebration. It was a few days early for the full moon, but they always try to fit it in when the maximum number can participate. Angie had read the evening's story to me, and we had a nice conversation about the things that brought up, so the Face-Time conversation was a fitting finale to the evening, which may explain partly why I had such a good day today.

Today has been a relatively good day, pain-wise. For some reason, I have just not been in pain today in the usual way, and I have to say that I am truly grateful for that gift. Today I got to have my shower (still able), changed the bandage on the liver stent (thanks to Angie), had Lauren from Home Care in to change the pain med port and do my weekly check-up, and got a chance to catch up on reading and writing so everything is looking good. Tomorrow should be interesting, as Angie got back from a successful little tune-up ride and everything is green lights for her to leave for competition tomorrow morning, and Linda will take me out there Saturday, we should be able to leave by noon and be there early afternoon, to see how it all went. I'm not sure why I'm so excited about it, but the renewal of competition has me revved up as well. And I just heard that Shawn is on his way to drop off the new and improved, and totally finished, version of the electric massage table, so that is just one more positive cog in my wheel. He is as much a perfectionist as I am.

Dale - May 20, 2016

While Shawn was here last night, I collapsed two or three times, once allowing myself a controlled drop gently to the floor and twice supported by Shawn. No damage any of those times, as I am learning how to protect myself quite a lot better as I understand what brings on the weakness. Angie and I had a nice cuddle on the couch last evening, followed by another decent night with only a little pain, and that's easily manageable. Five hours of good sleep with one minor interruption, followed by almost four hours more is certainly nothing to sneeze at (funny term). Angie is outside putting the finishing touches to everything for her competition, and I am so glad to hear that she is feeling positive on so many angles about both her participation in this event, and her state of readiness. We are both having some concerns about Shmu's condition, and how much time she has left as well, as she is having some trouble eating again, but on the other hand, this rain that is falling bodes well for what our other equines will eat this coming winter – there might actually be hay this year in our area!

Well, Angie and Deb were just putting the final touches in place in preparation for pulling out for the race tomorrow, and I chanced across a post from Mary B. announcing the cancellation due to weather of the Endurance event. Angie was able to go online and confirm that the event was cancelled, so we called it a very successful dry run to test all systems for readiness. The timeliness was amazing, as it saved them a drive that might have been to no purpose, and so now they can just focus on putting some things away and keeping the rest set up for their future training as they stay in 'event shape' for the future. Linda decided to head home so Mom wouldn't be alone tonight, and Angie and I had the day to just relax together.

Several days after my blog about blame, Jen D. wrote this today: "I've been thinking about this ever since Dale posted this. I realize that I hate blame. Nothing is ever solved in blame, often I tell my boys I don't care who did it, "Fix it!" A marriage counselor once said, as long as someone is saying, "you, you, you," they're never looking at themselves, and the part they played in the issue. Then I see myself and know I have work to do, learning to love and forgive again."

Dale - May 21, 2016

What is the nature of forgiveness? Can I just forgive someone without understanding this? I am drawn deeper into the well of all of the people I have the hardest time forgiving, including myself, as I try to understand this. So why are some people harder to forgive than others? I am starting to think it is not really a problem of how much hurt there was: although on the surface the ones that hurt the most are often the hardest ones to face up to, they are often also the most obviously needing of forgiveness. I want to forgive, because I recognize in myself the need to be forgiven. If I cannot forgive others without knowing their history and the reasons they were "mean" to me, how can I ever expect others to forgive me without knowing my history, and how will they ever hear my history without forgiving me at least enough to listen? I believe that the trouble between human beings and the trouble between nations is merely, then, a matter of degree. You did this to me (my belief or understanding of the situation, regardless of whether I am absolutely sure or not), and now you must make amends (regardless of whether you recognize that need or not), or I must force you to make amends (by whatever means possible) or, alternately, I must create a barrier that will prevent you from ever causing me that kind of pain again. That barrier means that I can protect myself from the pain you might cause me, but it also means that I prevent any possibility of receiving the enrichment that you could potentially bring into my life, and that potential was the reason for connection in the first place.

What is the value of forgiveness? The value of forgiveness is to open me up to any possibility of dialogue and enrichment, and that possibility of dialogue is what helps me to expose and understand the depths of my soul. Each person that I meet brings the chance to understand myself better, and that connects me more and more to the world I live in and my place as part of that world. I want to understand the depths of love, both as a 'lover' and as an object of love, and in love there is no room for blame, or as Brene Brown would say, for shame which is the ultimate goal, both inwardly and outwardly, of blame. I highly recommend the book "The Gifts of Imperfection" for anyone who is struggling with the blame/shame cycle. Also, the Netflix movie Angie and I watched last night triggered some thoughts on this subject: "Palm Trees in the Snow" is a subtitled movie shot mostly in Spanish, about Spanish colonial times in western Africa. It has some harsh and morbid themes, and some blatant sexuality for those who might be offended, but overall had many very valuable lessons in my opinion.

Suzanne W. - Thank you so much for your insights about this very touchy subject about forgiveness. I know I have forgiven my mom, but I am still unable to have any connections with her, because unfortunately, happiness comes within our soul and not from the outside world or someone else always trying to please you. To make you happy. She will never be happy regardless of what I do for her and it drains and sucks the life out of me. I hope you can find it in her heart to forgive yourself, we are not perfect, we are here to learn lessons and to try and improve and be aware(only when we are aware of the things we need to change) can we improve our life. Too many lessons to learn in this short time on this earth. We can only do what we can do and leave this planet a better person than we started as. Love you! Sending Big Hugs! You deserve to be at peace with yourself!

Dale - When we expect a response from another person over our action, we have to ask ourselves this question: "Who am I trying to change?" If the answer has any component of I'm trying to change their actions (or responses), then I think we have chosen a very difficult road, indeed. The only heart we can see clearly into at all is our own, and that only with effort and great willingness. The only thing that makes our Moms (or any other person we are trying to help) happy is their ability to forgive themselves for any hurt they have perceived themselves to cause, and we can encourage that but not create that. If I can forgive myself for any of my failures, and if I can learn to Love myself for all that I have done, and I can Love others just as they are without needing to change them at all, then I can be at peace. Love back to you, Suzanne.

Dale - May 22, 2016

Today was just a quiet day, a chance to soak in all the events of the week and enjoy a day alone with Angie, basking in her love, and sending her all the love I have left.

Angie

All the love that Dale "had left" was a lot. I always felt his love and I still do.

Dale - May 23, 2016

Too bad I never thought to put this in yesterday's note, but we weighed myself last night just to see where I am, and I'm now down to 107 lbs.. That's pretty light, by any standard. Quite frankly, I'm surprised I have the energy to read and write. I am, however, sleeping, and last night I got five hours of solid sleep, woke up to urinate, and then got another four hours. Energy fading slowly and quietly seems to be the path for me. I've also noticed that my eyesight is gradually weakening as well, both in quality and in quantity, but I've read that is fairly normal as well under these conditions.

Jocelyn is coming with Deb today to evaluate Mo at the next stage of her treatment plan, and Angie and I are both excited to hear how she sees his progress, as I have such hopes for Mo's ability to compete this year. I guess that's why I was so disappointed that he had to be pulled from the May long weekend endurance race, even before the weather conspired against the event. Hopefully, Angie will get a bit of a ride today on Dude without too much rain during the ride, so she can enjoy it more. I also have company coming today: Leah's dropping in to see me for a short visit, so I have that to look forward to.

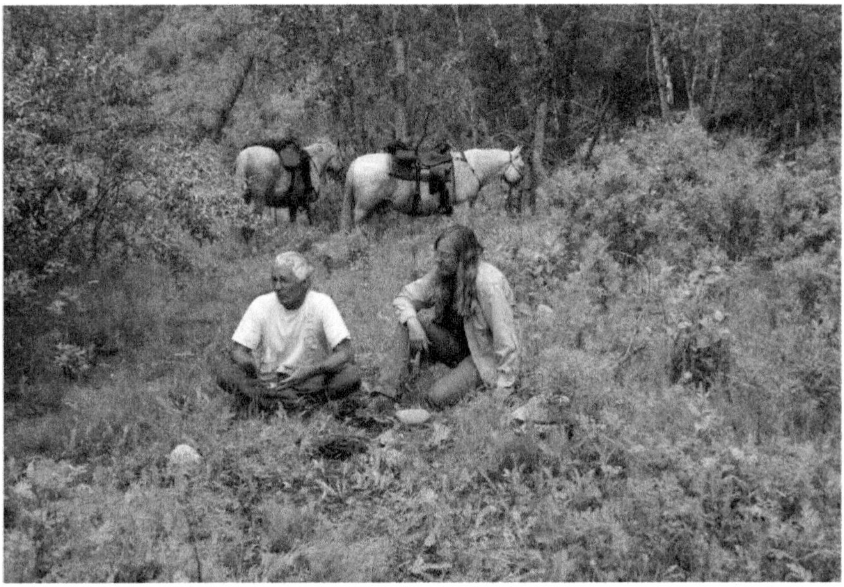

Dale, Angie, Mo and Dude several years ago, having lunch with friends out on the trail.

Nick Polizzi from The Sacred Science organization put up this poem this morning, and I thought it was beautiful enough to repeat:

Oh Great Spirit, Whose voice I hear in the winds, And whose breath gives life to all the world, Hear me! I am small and weak, I need your strength and wisdom.

Let me walk in beauty, and make my eyes ever behold the red and purple sunset.

Make me wise so that I may understand the things you have taught my people.

Let me learn the lessons you have hidden in every leaf and rock.

I seek strength, not to be greater than my brothers and sisters, but to fight my greatest enemy – myself.

So when life fades, as the fading sunset, my spirit may come to you without shame.

Karen D. - I take inspiration from your journals and I pray for the strength you have – when my time comes I fear I will be very cowardly.

Dale - If you allow yourself to live in fear, you create your own reality. Ask yourself what it is that you are really afraid of, and work on releasing that.

Brittany H. - Dale I could learn a thing or two from you my friend you made me really think.

Christine S. - So ein schönes, beruhigendes Gedicht! Ich bewundere Sie sehr, Mr. Pierce und ich bin sicher, dass Ihr Tagebuch ganz vielen Menschen Mut macht und die kleinen Alltagssorgen relativiert.

Translation - Such a beautiful, soothing poem! I admire you very much, Mr. Pierce and I am sure that your diary gives many people courage, and that their small, everyday problems are put into perspective. Hugs from Austria to you.

Dale - May 24 and 25, 2016

Monday Deb was supposed to come over with Josephina (not Jocelyn as earlier misreported) but in any case Deb came down with flu symptoms and decided to stay away in everyone's best interests. End result: no checkup for Mo, and even more sadly, no ride for Angie. Angie was, however, able to spend the afternoon reconnecting with another old friend from her coffee-truck days, Kerry. For me, Monday was a day of not much physical, mental or emotional change, and really nothing to report.

Tuesday: Physically, I'm just starting to feel more and more blocked up, so we decided to try an enema again after quite a long time without and I would have to say that finally got things moving. We cleaned me out and I feel a lot better moving forward, and I'm again surprised at how much better I feel at every level. I now weigh just a hair under 104 lbs., so that shows how little relative nourishment I'm getting, but I am doing the best that I can, and I'm still eliminating about a litre of fluids a day so I'm keeping the kidneys flushed and functioning. And yes, I'm using a pee bottle so I can keep some level of monitoring on the fluid intake and outgo.

Dennis dropped over for a bit in the early afternoon, to keep an eye on me and to keep me company while Angie and Deb evaluated Mo and then decided what to do. Sadly, based on his history and their evaluation, it looks like Mo's days as a distance horse are done, as a combination of old injuries and my inexperience and lack of time to spend with him last year during his rehabilitation year have just set him too far back for the things that can be done to work successfully. He can, however, be a decent short ride horse for the future, so at least there is that. And then Glory's freak accident seems to have put her out of contention as even a riding horse for the future, so now Angie and Deb are stuck with trying to figure out a mount for Deb to condition so that she can try some distance riding this year and I'm sure that they will figure something out.

In the meantime, Dennis and I spent the afternoon having a guy talk about things that could happen after I'm gone, and some of my concerns about Angie's future were assuaged, leaving me feeling quite a bit better on that front as well. Talking to Dennis about these things, and even some more around father/son stuff, really helped me to let go of more and more of my worries and cares around earthly affairs, and I can feel myself letting go of more and more of the things that are holding me here, in this life.

So, today is Angie's shopping day, and I have a new person going to sit with me from Respite care while she can go and get things done without having to worry about me falling and breaking something. I should be able to amuse myself while she's gone and we have plans for the next few days with company Thursday and my sister sitting with me Friday so Angie can get another ride in this week, get some yard work done, have the farrier over, and get her hair cut. It is a busy life we lead.

Terrence P. - Almost like ripples, do you think?

Dale - Sorry, Terry my cognitive powers seem to be fading a bit, I'm not following you this time. What are you referring to by ripples?

Terrence P. - I think that when we work through circumstances that are so monumental (as you are currently), there is a tendency for that energy contained therein, either positive or negative, to be transmitted to other areas of our lives where it has a measurable and quite possibly mysterious effect. Like with Mo and Glory, but also with family and friends, nothing happens in this connected universe without causing an effect of some kind, somewhere. I'm not an equine therapist by any means, but I do know their "mirroring" tendencies - that is they reflect their surroundings, their humans' emotions and circumstances. They are connected to you and I'm sure are affected by what's going on in your life! As we all are, indeed!

Daisy S. - Sending hugs to both you and Angie. And this lovely quote from Richard Bach; it keeps running through my head right now. "Don't be dismayed by good-byes. A farewell is necessary before you can meet again. And meeting again, after moments or lifetimes, is certain for those who are friends. "

Dale - May 26, 2016

On another note, I do continue to receive many heartwarming and encouraging messages from both clients and friends, as well as visits and offers of visits. Sometimes I think I forget to mention how blessed I feel on a continuing basis. Today has been a lovely day of introspection. I had a wonderful visit with Jen D. late this morning that reminded me of the importance and the beauty of the purely interpersonal connection that allows the soul of another person to shine through without any need to try to change the other person. People come into and out of our lives, holding us captive or merely sharing the love that they have been given to share, and I love that we are able to reconnect with people that have been a positive influence in our lives at will, and seemingly effortlessly. That is the relationship that we all, I believe, crave at the bottom of our hearts. As I just said to one of my dear friends, Love holds the power that overcomes all obstacles in life.

I've spent the day since answering emails, and listening to inspirational messages from some who have been very positive influences in my life, besides friends. The music of Enya, which I was introduced to in 05/06 by Angie and the Acupuncture Clinic, and still does not seem to lose its currency. The words of Brene Brown in some of her TED talks. There is always something to be picked up from listening to her, even if it is only amusement at her humor, including her seemingly very healthy self-directed humor. And then Doreen dropped in for a short visit with the gift of a heating pad with vibration to give me relief from lying in bed all day. I tried it out, and it will be wonderful to use from time to time. Thank you so much, Doreen. Then, after some time to think and write, my sister has arrived so that Angie can go and ride for a bit this afternoon, so she and I'll spend the afternoon together and then the evening with Angie.

Karen D. - It is wonderful that you have a circle of friends and family around you! You are blessed.

Jen D. -The best thing I did today was come see you. Thank you.

Dale - And, again, thank you so much for coming.

Jen D. - My pleasure. The drive was quite reflective and good for me! Up and Back. Thank you for yesterday.

I've been thinking ever since about our conversation about pain and the displacement of it. You helped me see that all these years I've carried pain, a broken heart, a broken home, a broken spirit. But when we talked about it, I realized that in my carrying it, I never put it on Jesus. I just tried to bury it, ignore it, deny it, and be stronger than it. I know that Christ has the ability to carry out infirmaries. I just never really leaned on the corner stone in that way. I love you Dale, thanks for your help. You are not "warehoused". You've helped me forever. I was wondering if Angie would make me a book mark, a skinny one, about 5 inches long. With a reminder of you on it. A picture? A poem? Seeing as how there will be no service for you, I'd like a physical memory. And if she'd send it to me. If she would please. Ask her nice lol. I'd like if for my bible. Maybe other people would like them as well? To another day with you. Jen

Jacki D. - I think of you every day! As your client I just want you to know how wonderful you are as a human being! I love reading your posts.

Kat I. - I'm getting such an insight as to what is important as all earthly concerns fall away. Some of us spend all our energy running away from ourselves.

Samantha J. - Thank you, as always Dale, for sharing such wisdom.

Dale - May 27, 2016

Yesterday evening was spent in the company of the gifted Tiiu McLim, who came out to give Angie and me a joint treatment, which turned out to be incredibly healing for both of us. There seems to never be a limit on the boundaries of self-discovery once I allow myself to open the door to possibilities, and so I find myself still learning, even as I lie here supposed to be dying. The aftermath of that treatment is another whole level of peace and letting go for me, as well as some insight into the roots of the cancer that is ushering me into the next aspect of my existence.

Today was a day of introspection and writing, and I was able to talk to my sister (who is staying over so that Angie can ride Saturday) and also to my mother by phone just to check a couple of things. It is really awesome to be able to get such a much clearer perspective on how things had been at the end of my Dad's life, and how clearly he had changed in some aspects (at least some aspects that truly mattered to me). Today my Mom gave me permission to leave, which had to have been incredibly hard for her to do, as I had come to the realization that I did actually want her permission, if not her blessing.

All in all, other than the fact that I am still here, this has been a very satisfying week. Angie got all her inside and outside chores done, and got some great rides in as well as was able to make meaningful plans for her distance riding goals this year, I've been able to reconnect with some significant people from my past, and I've made great progress in my journey. My mind is still sharp (although I am hearing from some corners that is both relative and debatable, LOL), my kidneys are still working, and I probably still weigh more than 100 lbs.

Terrence P. - Funny you mention the giving of permission. I did the same thing with Mom after she'd been paralyzed for about 8 years. I finally sat down and told her it was ok if she needs to go. We'd be fine! Shortly thereafter she passed.

Suzanne W. - I get what you're saying about the permission, I told my sister the same thing when she was sick with cancer. Not sure if it's said because we're now ok with what is happening or have come to terms that we are losing a piece of our life which we cherish with all our hearts! Or to just let our loved one know all will be ok! But very happy you're still here! The rain has stopped and the robins are singing again! Love ya! BIG HUGS as always! God bless you and Angie.

Tiiu M. - Xoxox thank you for sharing such an incredible experience with me. You and Angie are remarkable people and my wish for you is to be able to let go.

Tammie M. - When my mom was dying and in a coma hanging on, my brother told her that it was ok for her to go and at that moment he watched her take her last breath and she was gone home to the other side where my dad was waiting for her I was so happy to know that she had gone home but yet sad because I would miss her. Just as Rod and I will miss you too when you go!

Katrin S. - Thanks for sharing your Story.

Verda J. - Our dear Dale...I keep reminding you how much we love you but today as I read your amazing report I decided to add a bit more to tell you how much it means to be able to keep in touch even if only a little...We have always loved it when we are able to be with you and get one of your oh so special hugs and nearly always a whole lot of teasing which if you didn't tease I would think you didn't love me anymore and I know that could never happen!!! Our visit with you last year when we were in Alberta will always be among our most treasured memories and once again THANK YOU to you and your sweet Angie...I love the picture of me on that horse when in my Eighties...LOVE YOU MORE THAN YOU CAN EVER KNOW AND PRAY FOR YOU LOTS!!!!!

Marlene Q. - The sad fact is that you are more "ALIVE" than most of the people out there, including myself at times, we get so bogged down in our own messes, it's hard to see the way out. Sometimes I envy you as your journey has held many blessings. Just know your sharing this means a lot to those of us that love you and Angie.

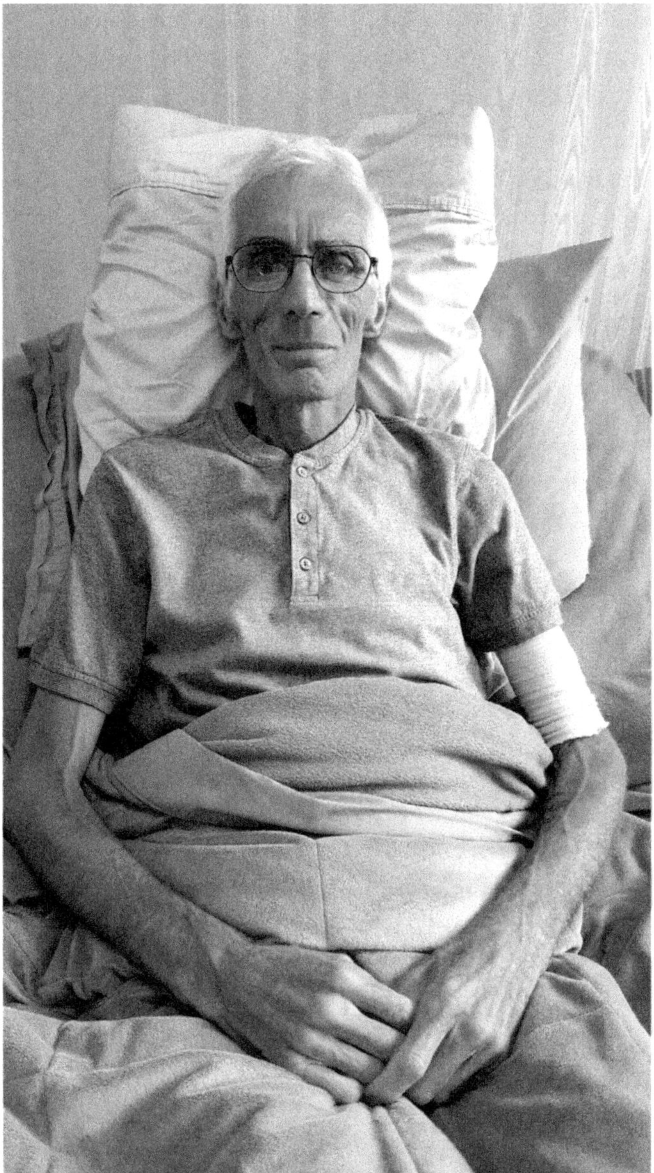

Dale - May 28 and 29, 2016

Saturday I had a wonderful visit with Wayne C., who was able to drive out and spend a bit of time with us here. Wayne is a like-minded soul that is so full of wisdom and is open and willing to share that wisdom, and I found both comfort and inspiration in his visit. I spent the early afternoon writing letters to people who I feel I still have unfinished business with, some of which will be sent and some of which are totally for me. After resting a bit, I was also able to spend an hour outside on the lawn swing in the sunshine, and then Angie and I were able to just spend some time together, and then I had a good night's sleep.

Sunday has so far been cleanup day. After all was said and done, I'm maintaining at 103 lbs. for some strange reason. Got my weekly bandage change, and now further quiet and reflection is all I expect out of today, and a continuation of closing up old matters so that I can feel comfortable that there is no unfinished business that I am leaving behind. Got to sit outside and nap in the sun off and on while Angie got in a bit of yard work this afternoon, then inside for a quiet evening before bed.

Dale - May 30, 2016

Monday. Somehow, the name of the day of the week doesn't have the same power it ever used to have, and yet there is still something evocative about that word. I just got word that my brother Jim is going to be able to stop by tomorrow between some appointments in the city and going back to Edson, so that is exciting. It will be nice to see him in person instead of just hear his voice on the phone. Also today I was able to write several letters closing off old business with people from the past. In the act of writing, I have found such a catharsis of release combined with the relief that none of these old things have any power over me any longer, as I am not holding old grudges or even any measurable mount of bitterness. Trying to find negative feelings to write about has left me feeling clear and cleansed. I thank the Universe for another gift this time has granted.

Dale - May 31 – June 1, 2016

End of May, and I can truly say that I never expected to see this day from this side of the veil. Yesterday, I felt like I finished any of the letters of apology or forgiveness that I wanted to write. Some of those were given to people, and some of those will be sent in some form after I pass, and some of those were, I guess, quite useful as exercises in releasing the power of thought in our own lives. Today, I'm going to write some letters of hope and encouragement to some people, and I sincerely hope that they will go out to a few friends who might be in need of such reminders. If you don't get one from me, then that must mean that I think you already have all of the hope and encouragement that I could possible offer you!

I had a lovely visit with my brother Jim in the afternoon and early evening, which allowed Angie to take care of more of the business regarding Cody's estate and also to get in a quick ride through the subdivision to keep Dude fit for the competition coming up in a week and a bit. It has amazed us how long the whole insurance process has taken for Cody, but we finally heard that almost six months from the day that Cody died (of natural causes) the insurance companies have finally begun to pay out the claims. Part of the problem seems to be the need for the Medical Examiners report, which is much more complicated in these circumstances than if it had been an accident. Anyway, Angie had to be able to focus on business for a bit without worrying about me, so that was a golden opportunity.

Then there is the case of Dude. He is such a finely tuned animal that Angie has brought to just the right condition for this season that barring a freak accident they should really have a great season together. I'm so proud of her, and so happy to see her make progress and ride so well. Also, because he is so finely tuned though, Angie has to keep his drive and push in line with regular contact reminding him of who the leader of his little herd really – and that is Angie, not Mo.

Anyway, back to my brother Jim. I really didn't expect to have him able to visit again before I checked out, so it was a very pleasant surprise to hear on Monday that he would be able to visit yesterday, between his scheduled work and health stuff. We have a good relationship, but most of it had been a relatively long-distance relationship, and I was surprised in the end at how much I wanted to just spend a little one-on-one time sharing old memories and what-not. It seems that there are always things that have been left unsaid, and face to face is a better way to evoke those feelings than most other methods. Also a chance to discuss feelings in a non-threatening environment.

Today I had Respite Care provided by Home Care. That allowed Angie to go into the city and shop, get herself a massage, and generally look after some of the things that she needed to do to keep us operating out here. Another blessing. I also had a lovely visit with Cheryl, who was able to spend some time with me and chat, as well as doing some Reiki on me, and a little Reflexology. More blessings. I'm reminded of my friend Laurie L. up in Radway whose favorite saying is something like 'how did I ever get to be so lucky', except that I translate lucky as blessed, and I know how – we are all born with the innate ability to be blessed. Our biggest problems are that we continuously view the world as our problem and our troubles as our enemies when instead we can choose to view them as our opportunity and our teachers. But who teaches us to think in that opportunistic way as we grow up? Who encourages us to open our minds and our hearts to the possibilities? Something for us all to think about.

Angie

Dale was being somewhat subtle about Dude and I in his post. What he failed to mention was that I had come off twice, within a few weeks, while riding in the bird sanctuary. We have a very large population of moose, which horses are deathly afraid of. Dude has seen enough moose to not lose his mind if he sees one in the distance. However, when I'm training for competitions I am moving down the trail at a good speed, usually at a brisk trot around eight to ten miles an hour. Problems arise when our presence on the trail surprises moose that are browsing in the bush, causing them to bolt, which creates quite a racket. This sudden racket causes Dude to do an "about-face", known in the equine world as a rollback. If you've heard of Newton's first law of motion - sometimes referred to as the law of inertia. An object at rest stays at rest and an object in motion stays in motion with the same speed and in the same direction unless acted upon by an unbalanced force. And that is what often happens to me, Dude spins and heads off in the other direction without me. I can't really blame him for that reaction; it is his instinct for self-preservation in action, especially when we are out there by ourselves. The best I can do is to be prepared with my mind and body, at all times. I was not injured either time that I met the dirt; scraped by thorn bushes the first time and bruised the second time. At my age, I consider these incidents as bone-density tests.

Karen D. - Very true Dale it seems most of us live our lives dealing with day to day things and never look any further...

Laurie L. - Sure make me cry!! Your journey has been a treasure to witness and be a part of (how did I get so blessed!?!

Terrence P. - Fortunately, some actually are able to rise to the challenge of opportunistic growth despite our initial programming. Although I'm sure we've raised enough eyebrows on the other side as our actions befuddle the universe. "How did those humans actually manage to crawl out of their hole?"

Suzanne W. - Dale you certainly have a way with words. You've opened my eyes to so many ways to look at life, to forgive and how to be able to forgive myself. I've been so blessed through my life even through all the difficult times. I've had Angels looking out for me. I know Angels are looking out for you as well. Love ya! Sending the Biggest Hugs you can muster.

In response to a post where an older generation person complained, with some justification, that the current generation wasn't giving enough credit for the good things being done by them without a "green policy" back in the day, I posted this:

Dale - Yikes! A lot of truth there, but why so bitter? We shouldn't be slamming people for learning the lessons that our generation taught them, any more than we should be bitter at our parents for learning the lessons that we picked up from them, about human dignity and freedom. Each generation wants the world to be a better place for the next generation, and yet we are always surprised when the lessons we try to teach are interpreted in a different way than we foresaw. If our world was so perfect, why did our generation try to change it at all?

Tammie M. - You've got a good point there Dale. Our world will never be perfect. We would run out of things to experience if man didn't keep changing things. Life is all about experiencing and learning how to deal with each experience that we have. All of the influences and experiences in our lives, make us who we are.

Dale - June 2, 2016

Today has been a busy day, almost to the point of too busy. I had my biweekly enema and shower today: biweekly as I'm eating so very little that cleansing twice a week is serving me very well. Basically, all of that takes up most of the morning. Lauren from Homecare came after lunch to switch my subcutaneous port from the left arm to the right for the week, and give me my weekly checkup, and by all reports I am doing very well. Then my sister Linda arrived to sit with me so Angie could ride with Deb this afternoon, and Angie could cut the grass again tomorrow morning, all without Angie having to worry about watching me every moment, as I may be that close at all times to checking out. Later this afternoon, our friend Colleen will be stopping by for a brief visit, and then our friend Larry is coming for supper as he has become a weekly bachelor for a while. Then, just to top things off, I'm waiting to hear from another friend who may be stopping in to pick up some stuff to be delivered to another friend in Camrose. No time today for meditation or almost even contemplation.

Dale - June 3 and 4, 2016

Thursday night my sister Linda stayed over so that she could look after me a bit longer while Angie got some things ready for the weekend. It is always a blessing when she is here because she gives such marvelous foot rubs, and those little things are the magic that makes life wonderful. Then Shawn came out to visit and pick up the hydraulic massage table for delivery in Camrose, and have lunch with us, thus finishing off another big chunk of business. Shawn has been so good to us, I'm sure Cody would be proud of him! While Shawn was finishing up, my nephew Rob dropped in between business in Wetaskiwin and heading home for a short but very lovely visit. We used to always think that we were so isolated here, but it no longer seems so based on the number of visitors we are getting, and again and again I am feeling blessed by how many people care enough to come out and see me. Finally, Harry and Lori arrived from Calgary to spend the evening with Angie and me. I had a short nap after they arrived, and then they brought out and cooked (to perfection) the bacon-wrapped ribeye steaks that they had prepared for supper. We later went out and sat by the fire on the south end of the house for the evening while we had a marvelous visit, talking about old times and what the future will bring and the things that we are all learning while I am going through this process. They were able to stay overnight and leave this morning for safe driving, so we all felt good about that, and it was a most marvelous visit.

Lots of contemplation time today, and I've been thinking some more about the forgiveness that I might still have to do, and what it is that I still think might be in the way of some of it. I believe that to a large part I'm still tempted by the wonderful stories that are running around in my head. Let's face it, and please bear with me because I think this is true of most of us, I still think of myself as a pretty good story teller, whether on the subject of fact or fiction. The stories that I have built up around why my life is exactly what it is have really served me very well thus far in explaining my motivations for both actions and feelings, whether the stories are based on things that I have figured out myself or things that have been told to me by others, and so my task now seems to be to examine the basis of those stories to see if they are true stories or not. As I find myself examining those stories, I find that I have more often than I like, I have allowed convenient untruths to creep in and make the stories more palatable to me – not big things always, but just simple things that smooth the edges. And those are the things that I want to erase. The story does not have to be easy, but it needs to be true.

Kat I. - In telling stories you cannot tell the absolute truth. In a series of events, one detail will have less weight as it happens, but end up having profound relevance at the end. The small truth has a back story that needs to be told but it is likely only speculation. Memories fail. This doesn't mean we have deliberately altered the facts, but we experience things through our own filter. "Smoothing out" is part of a writer's craft. The alternative to that is being boring.

Suzanne W. - Yes, you are a wonderful story teller, I sure wish I could put into words how I feel or try to explain myself so eloquently as you. Sometimes as you said & I'm very certain most if not all people have conveniently adjusted some of their truths to either make themselves feel better or make someone else feel better as well. Definitely something to reflect on. Trying to protect yourself from the hurt the truth may cause. Love you! Would love to come over & give you a Big Hug but I don't want to intrude.

Daisy S. - I am quite certain there is no absolute truth. Perception, while not everything, is the best we have & while it can be changed some times that doesn't make it more or less true. This may be true of not only the grand abstracts but also the details & stories of our lives. In the end when we discover we are never actually going to KNOW the truth we can chose to believe what makes us happy. Your courage shines in every word.

Chris E. - I read a book called "A Million Miles in a Thousand Years" about a young guy who didn't like his story & so he changed it. I too liked my "story", brought me lots of sympathy and allowed me to "live small". So I changed my story too. And the amazing thing I found for myself was that it also changed the story I had always been telling myself and others. It softened the edges, blurred the lines, and the perception of what was changed too. I can say I am honestly grateful for all that happened because it's made me who I am today and I'm pretty darn proud of who I am!

Suzanne W. - I may have to pick up that book! Thank you for sharing.

Dale - June 5, 2016

Today has been ablution day. There, I have been resisting using that word, but it is such a cool word that I finally gave in and used it. Ablutions. The four holy "sh"s of the manly life: shit, shave, shampoo and shower! And I feel great, even though I officially weigh less than 100lbs. for the first time ever (well, in over 50 years)! We went outside and had our coffee on the deck in the sun this morning, and it felt just awesome. Dying in the summer is alright, as I got to just sit and absorb the green grass, the sunshine, the birds singing, bees buzzing, flowers blooming, plants growing. The only thing missing was the two geldings grazing just across the rail fence from the deck, but then I got to experience that later today when Dennis and Mary-Lynn stopped by for a few hours, we spent some time this afternoon on the back deck with the horses free grazing in the yard, and then barbequed smokies over a fireplace fire after they were put away. All in all, this has been a great weekend.

Chalane H. - Blessings and love to you and Angie. I will always remember you. Grateful.

Terrence P. - Embracing you (AND me!).

Suzanne W. - When my time comes, I certainly hope I can leave this earth with as much grace & elegance as you. I feel so privileged for allowing me to be part of your incredible journey with all the people who care and love you so! Sending you the biggest hugs ever! Yes! I would want my last breath to be outside while I take in all the sounds & beauty of summer.

Shawn S. - Sounds awesome man.

Dell P. - Life's little pleasures turn out to really be the big ones. So nice to experience them.

Tammie M. - You picked the right time to go, summer is so much nicer than winter.

Verda J. - Dearest Dale. You have such a wonderful way with words! God be with you every moment of every day.

Kathy N. - Hi Dale, I just wanted to let you know I'm thinking of you. Sending all my positive energy, hugs and prayers. I know you must not be up for any writing and that is understandable, so I thought I would write to you. You continue to inspire me. To have gratitude for each day, to forgive with all my heart, to let love heal, to be good, to do good. Peace be with you.

Dale - June 15, 2016

I see there has been a long gap between my last post and this one, and I suspect that is because I'm rapidly reaching the end of my posting days. I want to take this opportunity to thank everyone who has followed these posts and who has found some small tidbits of value and expressed them back to me. Those expressions have given me such a feeling of worth in the last few months, a feeling that I'm not just churning out stuff to fill my remaining time meaninglessly, but perhaps even contributing meaningfully to the overall raising of the level of consciousness in this world I will so soon be leaving.

Another thing I wanted to say for sure was a big shout out to all of Angie and my friends in the world of TRAC and ERA for making Angie feel so welcome at the Caroline event this past weekend. You guys all understand the importance of horses and riding to the sanity (and even physical health) of someone in Angie's position, and even your ability to just let her be there enjoying what we both loved so much, lending an air of normalcy to the craziness in her life, fills both of our hearts with joy and love for you all. Angie is also so looking forward to the Devon ride this weekend (as am I to hearing about it), which has always been one of our favorites, because of the trail, the people, the atmosphere, and because it is so close to home.

I would also specifically like to thank all of my clients and colleagues from my days in Camrose, Tofield and Edmonton clinics as I've tried to find my niche in the world of health and healing. Every one of you (yes, every one) has been a teacher to me, as much as I've ever been a teacher, helper or healer to them, and in some cases even more. So many of you have turned into dear and cherished friends that have been treasures in my life right until the end, whether we have spoken regularly or not in the last little while.

Another group of really important people in my life, certainly not least and maybe not last, is family. I've certainly been given a renewed sense of the concept of family and what that constitutes and what that means, whether by birth or acquisition. And of course one of the most important parts of family has been my soulmate, my lover, the igniter of my heart, my wife Angie. To have received the gifts that she has brought to my life, at any time in my life, feels like such a miracle that I am often simply overwhelmed with joy, love and a sense of peaceful bliss that my life could be so fulfilled.

Dale crossing the Pembina River on Mo in 2012.

I'd like to close with one final thought about looking at others, and how we tend, as humans, to divide their characters into positive and negative characteristics like good and bad, or uplifting or not, or even weakness and strength, and why choice of wording matters in describing it that way instead of some other way. I'd like you each to consider, just for a moment, how the flavours of those words leads us, often quite subtly into an easiness with judgement.

Barbara M. - Dale: I only got to spend a short period of time with you at Marlene and Roy's several years ago. The courage and grace you have shown during the past months is an inspiration for all of us.

Jennifer S. - Big hugs Dale! Thank you so much. :)

Holly S. - Sending love to you and Angie. I've been following your posts religiously, and you really have had an impact. After reading your posts, I'm reminded to "stop and smell the roses", savour the relationships I have, be kind, and to just enjoy life. I thank you for that. Your bravery throughout your journey has been truly inspiring.

Kimberly Mc - You will live on forever in my mind!

..With Jin Shin Do, connecting with clients through the effects of massage, speaking your mind in a genuine way, fun game nights, and the ability to take something really complex & simplifying in order to understand and connect with others about wild concepts in the world. These are things in life that remind me of you. And so many others, too!

I will always, always remember the life lessons you have taught me. Being unapologetic and bold - I have never met anyone like you and I thank you for showing me that any possibility can be available depending on how you look at it - Sitting with pain in a way that you aren't resisting the sensation, for example. Big things!

Love you very much.

Rodney M. -You truly have inspired me with your journey of life Dale. Your words of wisdom and love are greatly appreciated my friend. I will miss your postings that have inspired so many. Sending my love to you and Angie. I'm sure we will reconnect on the other side someday. Big Hugs

Angie

My darling Dale, I did not express myself with words about how I felt near the end. All of my love and dedication to you was expressed through caring for you physically. We had long ago discovered that service was our language of love. I've been told by health care workers and so many others that I did an amazing job looking after Dale. It means nothing. As a rule I take pride in my work but knowing that I did a "good job" doesn't seem to cut it. Perhaps, even though I know better, some part of me feels like I failed. I know that I couldn't have done more... but still.

I too feel like my life was fulfilled. I had known you for over 10 years and loved you as long, even though at the beginning we were only friends. You were my Anam Cara:

The Meaning of Anam Cara:

Anam Cara refers to the Celtic spiritual belief of souls connecting and bonding.

In Celtic Spiritual tradition, it is believed that the soul radiates all about the physical body, what some refer to as an aura. When you connect with another person and become completely open and trusting with that individual, your two souls begin to flow together. Should such a deep bond be formed, it is said you have found your Anam Cara or soul friend.

Your Anam Cara always accepts you as you truly are, holding you in beauty and light. In order to appreciate this relationship, you must first recognize your own inner light and beauty. This is not always easy to do. The Celts believed that forming an Anam Cara friendship would help you to awaken your awareness of your own nature and experience the joys of others.

According to John O'Donahue, an accomplished Irish poet, philosopher and Catholic priest, "...You are joined in an ancient and eternal union with humanity that cuts across all barriers of time, convention, philosophy and definition. When you are blessed with an anam cara, the Irish believe, you have arrived at that most sacred place: home."

Angie

On June 17 I set out for Devon to take part in the Ron Janzen Memorial endurance race. This ride honours the life of a wonderful man who was dedicated to his family and the sport of endurance riding. His family are the most supportive folks out there and have been there for me throughout this time, as have many others involved in the sport. This was one of our favourite rides and Dale did not want me to miss it. We knew he was close to the end. There was no denying it. The morning that I left I played "Just Like Them Horses" by Reba Macintyre and we had a very special moment ... just in case. If you're not familiar with the song I suggest you locate the video on YouTube and grab some tissue. Reba sang it at her dad's funeral. Somehow I think we both knew that he wouldn't leave without me being there at his side. And we were right. He was still there on Sunday, but he was in pretty rough shape at this point.

He'd been having trouble with his eyes because the hydro-morphone was affecting his ability to close them. He usually slept with them open which was somewhat disconcerting at first. I felt like a vulture at times, checking for breathing, watching for movement ... waiting. Between Friday and Sunday when I returned Dale's eyes were developing large quantities of mucus. We had previously received a solution to help keep his eyes lubricated but this was another issue altogether. Several times a day I would gently clean his eyes so that he could see more clearly.

I changed his bandaging on Friday morning before I left while his sister Linda was there to watch, perhaps I had a premonition? Later that day bile started leaking directly out of the stoma (hole in his side) rather than draining through the tube and into the bag. Linda was able to change the dressing and creatively stop it from leaking into the bedding. On close examination I noticed that there were small holes in the tube. When I questioned Dr. Hackett about it (a month later) he informed me that there are holes in the last 6 inches of tubing, which is meant to be inside the liver. Apparently the body will naturally try to expel the stent and tubing and because Dale was well past his "expiry date" that's what was happening.

On Monday morning (June 20) Dale woke me at 5:30, "Baby, please make some coffee and get me a shot, but not a big one, we need to talk and I want to be coherent". He emphasised, once again, that he was "ready to go" and he hinted at the possibility that I could somehow help him with that. It wasn't a complete surprise, we had talked about it as an emergency solution, if the pain became unbearable. He was also terrified of going back to the hospital, he wanted more than anything to die at home. I promised him that I would not send him to the hospital and that I would not let him be in agony. I also told him that I would not consider such a thing simply because what we were going through was so hard. Having been around horses for so many years, and having pets, I'm no stranger when it comes to "the right thing to do". It's never an easy decision with animals but can you imagine when it's a person you love more than anything in the world? Interestingly, the assisted dying bill was passed in Canada on June 17.

Dale had an urgent need for the commode later that morning so I quickly fetched it from the other room and was trucking down the hallway with it when I rammed it into a doorjamb which subsequently rammed my already wrecked knee to the point that I nearly collapsed. I did however manage to get it there on time and Dale had what seemed to be a never ending bowel movement. Later that day Dale had a "little accident" in his boxers. He was losing the sensation that would warn him of impending poop. Not a big deal really, but then it happened again, and again. I remembered that I had once received a sample package of diapers in the mail (sometimes it pays to be a packrat, you never know right?). It was a pretty tight fit but Dale was barely 90 lbs.at this point so I could make them work. We also decided to discontinue the laxatives immediately LOL. Lauren brought us some Depends the next day so from there on in I had a 90 lb. baby. A very LARGE challenge indeed! Now I suppose many of you feel that I could spare the details, and leave out this gruesome chapter. Dale specifically asked me not to "spare his dignity". He wanted it ALL to be said. What's the point in sharing an experience like this, and then leaving out, or glossing over the morbid details. If you are squeamish I suggest you skip over the rest of this paragraph (how politically correct of me to insert the appropriate warning). For quite some time, Dale had been enjoying a coffee in the morning but he wasn't finishing his cup before it became cold so I came up with a solution that pleased him greatly. I blended his coffee with ice cream and created a "frappe-cino". He loved it. Now for the gross part, it looked about the same coming out as it did going in but ... OK never mind, I'll spare you, but you get the point.

Dale's mom and sister had stayed until late in the day the previous Sunday wondering if perhaps that was "the day". You see, they had also become vulture like. On Friday, June 24 they came up for the day on a premonition of Linda's but that was also not "the day". It was their last chance to have a visit and as I remember Dale could still speak at that point although it was becoming more and more difficult.

On Saturday our friend Cheryl S. came out for the day, I was planning to go for a ride while she stayed with Dale. I did not go, I was afraid to leave. She did Reiki for Dale and the three of us spent the day listening to music, crying, laughing, and remembering. It was a great day really, very emotional for all of us. Cheryl left around supper time, she had a client in Camrose that she'd already delayed by an hour in order to spend more time with us.

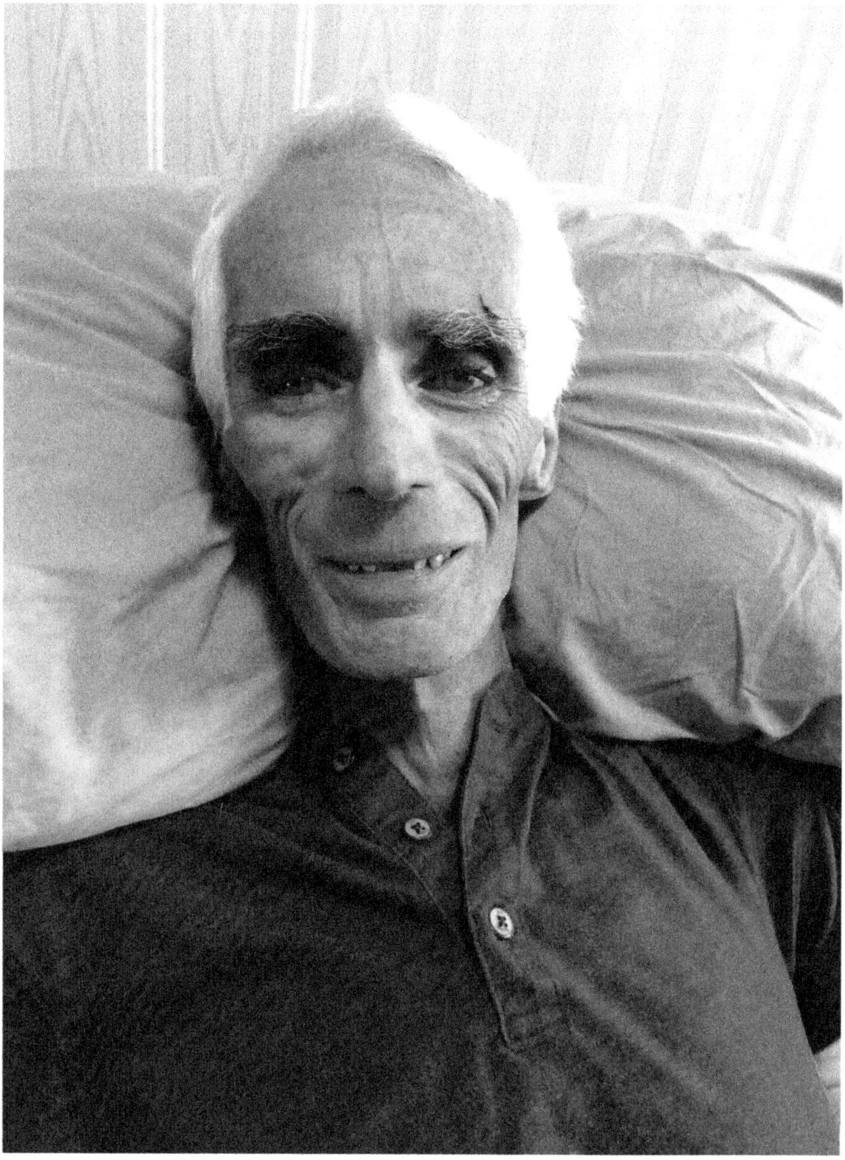

June 23, 2016 - This is the last picture taken of Dale.
He still had that special smile.

There was no question that Dale's time here was rapidly coming to an end. His feet had begun turning purple and there were other parts of his body that were showing signs to indicate that his body was shutting down. Although his body was icy cold, in his experience he felt fiery hot. Ice packs and cold cloths provided some relief. I was told that as the body shuts down the blood concentrates in the heart and brain areas which can cause the perception of extreme heat. He did not have the strength to speak although he could still whisper. He could not drink but I kept his mouth moist with swabs provided by our invaluable homecare nurse, Lauren. He complained of pain and was continuously asking for more hydro-morphone. He kept saying he needed to "get out". I knew what he was asking, but being faced with it right then and there rather than just discussing it was another matter entirely. Let me ask you, what would YOU do?

It was now becoming increasingly difficult for me to cope. I called my friends Dennis and Mary-Lynn who had been "on call" for me since May and they came as soon as they could. We sat with Dale and I took care of him, and they took care of me. All the preparation in the world cannot prepare you for someone you love so much to depart this world. At midnight I was totally exhausted on all levels, I could not sit there any longer and decided that I had to lie down and get some rest. My friends stayed the night and also went for some shuteye. I felt awful leaving Dale's side but I was done. I was only a few feet away so he easily could call me if he needed me. I'd been sleeping with one eye open for the past month or two anyway. I awoke at 4:20 with the horrible thought that Dale might've slipped away while I slept. I lay there for a few minutes shaking when I heard him clear his throat, Hallelujah! He was still alive! I quickly got to his side and did what I could for him.

As I sit here re-telling the tale on Dale's well used laptop, I find it hard to recall just what was said during those early hours. And some parts yet to come are even more blurry, at least when it comes to recalling the things that I said. Perhaps in the end it really doesn't matter what we say, what matters most are the feelings in our hearts. The Love we feel and share with others. The Beatles said it best: "And in the end the love you take is equal to the love you make". That lyric had such a profound effect on me in 1970 that I painted it on my bedroom door. I admit that it had an equally profound effect on my parents which was not nearly as philosophical.

Dale never lost his sense of humour, even in his last hour. While I was in the kitchen with Mary-Lynn, who was kindly preparing our breakfast, Dale beckoned to Dennis who was sitting with him, to come closer. He used his middle finger to do this, and if you can, imagine how thin and skeletal his hands were. Dennis thought Dale needed something; a moist swab, a cold cloth or maybe something else. Because Dale could only whisper Dennis had to get in real close to hear him say "Dirty Rotter!" You can only imagine the surprise Dennis felt upon hearing that. Now I know that Dale had nothing but the utmost respect for Dennis so I'm sure he was not implying that Dennis was a dirty rotter. I believe he was trying to communicate how he felt about the circumstances. For lack of a better term it SUCKED! And Dale wanted to express that sentiment to Dennis in a humorous and unforgettable way.

After breakfast we assumed our positions in Dale's room and proceeded to wait. It really was a never ending thing this waiting, for all of us. We weren't there very long when I was strongly compelled to play "Just Like Them Horses", it was after all the perfect song for us. As soon as it started Dale got a big smile on his face, we both loved the song. When it finished, I played a Dan Gibson's Solitudes album called "Angel's Embrace". I've enjoyed that album for many years and Dale had it in his massage music collection. It evokes a calm and peaceful, even romantic, feel. Within a minute or two Dale's breathing changed. He was gasping for air and we knew that the process of dying had begun, the waiting would soon be over, but not nearly as quickly as I would have liked.

By this time Dale's eyes were no longer the gorgeous baby blues we all remember. They were a cold grey and appeared not to be seeing anything, at least not what we were seeing. I was holding his hand and speaking to him, as I said before I cannot recall any of what I was saying and neither could my friends. He stared at me with those cold grey eyes and I held his gaze. His mouth was gaping as he struggled to breathe, after a few minutes the breath became shallow and I expected it to be over soon. I was mistaken. The gasping began again followed by shallow breathing. This cycle repeated itself several times. At one point I recall saying "will this ever end?" and also saying, "it seems as though his soul is gone and it's his body that is hanging on". I was correct on the first point, it did eventually end but he was definitely still aware. He raised the hand that I was holding and squeezed it, I believe to let me know he was indeed still there. Then, after 30 minutes he shuddered. It's hard to describe but he sort of rolled his shoulders like he was literally shedding his body. He did it twice and then he was gone. There was no doubt. I did check for signs which confirmed what I already knew. At 10:30 on June 26, 2016, Dale was gone.

So ends that chapter and so ends a life. What's left now is "life after Dale". I must say that at first, after the initial shock and sadness wore off I felt relief. I felt relief for him and for me. That lasted nearly a week. Then I saw a man from behind that, for a split second, made me think it was Dale. And it happened several more times. It's as if some part of the psyche misses someone so much that it's in search of them. I guess that's when it set in for me, the overpowering sense of loss. And so begins the process of grieving, the never ending cycle of up and down. Thankfully I have a to-do list that will keep me busy and I have my horses to keep me "in the moment".

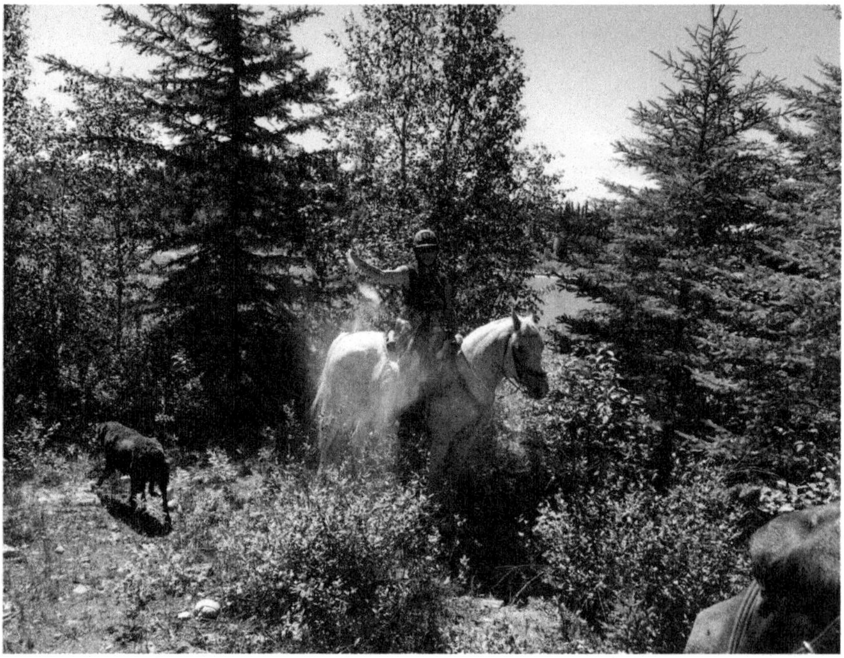

Angie on Dude, spreading a bit of Dale's and Cody's ashes in the Ministik Bird Sanctuary, a magical place where Angie and Cody rode when he was a young boy, and where Dale and Angie spent most of their time training for competitions. We felt so blessed to have this magnificent place to ride.

Acknowledgements

I'd like to begin with acknowledging every person, event or circumstance that gave us an opportunity for growth. During our many years together Dale and I tried to learn from it all, and I say tried because it's not easy, and neither of us had attained enlightenment. It's a human tendency to push away the things that are unpleasant. Dale's work in acupressure brought him to the realization that these unpleasant occurrences linger in the body, mind and soul, if they are not dealt with.

As for the people that helped us on our journey with cancer, I'd like to recognize a great many and can only hope that I leave no one out.

I will be forever grateful to all of the following:

The medical staff who put their efforts into Dale's comfort, there are so many whose names we never knew but we felt their kindness and compassion.

The doctors who went above and beyond, the fabulous Dr. Steinke who spent hours researching and never stopped searching for an answer, Dr. Zepeda, Dr. Gutfreund and especially the exceptionally compassionate Dr. Hackett who made things as convenient as possible for us.

Our awesome home care nurse, Lauren, we couldn't have kept Dale at home without her. She helped us through the worst of times, and in so many ways. And, the several respite care workers who came to be with Dale every week, while I ran into town to do errands.

The many practitioners, of all kinds, who offered their services in the way of treatments. In no particular order, Cheryl, Chris, Paula, Sabrina, Kimberley, Kim, Tiiu, Carol, Chantal and Inge.

Our family; Dale's Mother Helen, Sisters Linda and Laura, Brother Jim, Wilf, Rob and Denielle. Angie's half- Brother Peter, from Austria and step-Daughter Holly in Ontario. A special thank you goes out to Linda who went above and beyond to make it possible for me to go to distance riding competitions as well as train for them. And especially for the foot rubs she gave to Dale.

Our close friends Dennis and Mary-Lynn, Harry and Lori, Larry and Doreen, Marlene and Roy, Jerry and Patti, Deb, Dell, Jean, Colleen, Harriet, Linda, Kimberley and Jake, Tammie and Rod, Colleen and Ken, Tina and Henry, Daisy, Chris, Terry, and Cody's friends who are all like sons to me now: Josh, Shawn, Robin, Ryan, and Lane. And all those whom I may not have mentioned but who also offered caring gestures.

Special thanks to all the generous people who contributed to our financial well-being during a very difficult time. We could not have kept Dale at home if I'd have been working at a job outside the home.

Dale's clients, who supported him before and during the journey. I know how much he meant to you but you likely have no idea how much you meant to him.

Our distance riding friends who totally understand the role that horses play in keeping us grounded, and in the moment. That being said, I appreciate my horse Dude for the many hours of companionship and learning opportunities that he continues to offer.

All of our Facebook friends! You supported us and engaged with us throughout the journey. You gave Dale a purpose when he might've felt there was no longer any reason to be here.

You all made incredible contributions in so many ways, and I will always treasure your love and friendship.

Biography

Dale Pierce became a registered massage therapist in 2006. He had previously worked in computers, and he was a journeyman electrician. With massage, at the age of 53, he had finally found his calling. Following his massage training he took a two year program in Jin Shin Do® Bodymind Acupressure® and in 2012 he completed his certification as a teacher. Dale also studied Reiki and took all four levels up to master practitioner.

He met his wife Angie in 2005 while working together at an acupuncture clinic. The two became friends immediately. In 2007, Dale joined Angie on her 40 acre horse farm. Dale always had a love for horses which grew stronger and stronger over time. Trail riding was the couple's favorite pastime and in 2013 they began distance riding as a sport. In a matter of a few years the two had likely covered about 2,000 miles together on their beloved mounts, a pair of full brothers that Angie raised. They married in 2014 mounted on their beautiful white Arabians, JF Khosmic Connection a.k.a. Mo and JF Independantly a.k.a. Dude. Mo is steadfast, solid, charming, handsome and sometimes a bit stubborn… just like Dale. Dude on the other hand, is high strung, flighty, loving, pretty and sometimes a bit willful… just like Angie. Horses have always played an important role in Angie's life, for over 10 years she has worked in equine-assisted therapy where horses (and other equines) assist people in understanding themselves more fully.

In the spring of 2015 the couple opened their own massage clinic in Edmonton, Alberta, realizing a dream that they'd shared for many years. At the end of 2015 Dale was diagnosed with terminal cancer.

https://dalesjourney.com/

CPSIA information can be obtained
at www.ICGtesting.com
Printed in the USA
LVOW06*1821071216
516085LV00008B/13/P

9 781773 023250